BECOMING CULTURALLY RESPONSIVE EDUCATORS

5 Necessary Action Steps

Jahkari H. Taylor

© 2023 by Jahkari H. Taylor

All rights reserved. No portion of this book may be reproduced, stored in a retrieval system, or transmitted in any form or by any means—electronic, mechanical, photocopy, recording, scanning, or other – except for brief quotations without permission of the publisher.

1. Education 2. Culturally 3. Responsive 4. Educators

I. Title. II. Title: Becoming Culturally Responsive Educators

Published in the United States of America.

PURPOSE PUSHERS

Also Available from Jahkari "JT" Taylor

OVERCOMING BURNOUT
Daily Devotionals to Inspire Teachers
JAHKARI H. TAYLOR

Relational Teaching
Connection is the Key!
Jahkari H. Taylor

7 Traits Of A "Teacher With A Purpose!"
Jahkari H. Taylor

T.R.U.E. L.E.A.D.E.R.S. LEAD!
"Exhibiting Character and Embracing Commitments"
By Jahkari H. Taylor

The R.A.P. Challenge
Lyrics and Literature
Jahkari H. Taylor

EQUITY ON PURPOSE
The H.E.L.P. GUIDEBOOK
JAHKARI H. TAYLOR

Dedication

This book is dedicated to the countless researchers who came before me. Thank you for being persistent, relentless, and courageous in your attempts to do what is best for students, families, and communities. I am always encouraged and inspired when I think about the sacrifices you made as you labored to help educators better understand the needs of culturally diverse learners. As an emerging educational researcher, I truly stand on the shoulders of giants.

This book is also dedicated to the educators who cultivated me with love, instilled confidence in me through high expectations, and empowered me to believe in myself through words of affirmation and validation. Now, more than ever, the world needs "teachers with a purpose" to enter schools with a mission to help young people recognize their inherent brilliance.

Prelude - Clarifying Culture

Before we begin to engage in this conversation about *Becoming Culturally Responsive Educators,* I would like to establish a common foundation and address a few misconceptions about the term "culture." I believe culture is one of the most complex and difficult-to-define words in the English language. Due to the limits of this brief book, I do not seek to provide an exhaustive definition of culture. However, I do seek to establish a general understanding of culture that I believe is necessary for educators working with culturally diverse youth. Whether we are aware or not, our understanding of culture will impact how we engage in culturally responsive practices.

Defining Culture

Culture is an umbrella term that often represents many aspects and characteristics associated with how a group of people lives. Although many people confuse culture with race, culture is much more complicated than race. Dr. Tyrone Howard (2020), author of *Why Race and Culture Matter in Schools*, stated, "Culture is not bound exclusively by one's race, ethnicity, or place of origin, but is shaped by a myriad of factors (p. 53)."[1] Additionally, according to Saifer et al. (2011), culture

> includes the behaviors, actions, practices, attitudes, norms, values, communication styles, language, etiquette, spirituality, concepts of health and healing, beliefs, and institutions of a racial, ethnic, religious, or social group. Culture is the lens through which we look at the world. It is the context within which we operate and make sense of the world (p. 9).[2]

Human history has taught us that culture has always been central to human existence and human behavior. According to Saifer et al. (2011), "culture moves and motivates us ('makes us tick')" (p. 10).[3] For this reason, educators must be able to see culture as an instructional asset to move the academic needle forward and improve outcomes for diverse students. Research shows that students' academic and behavioral performance improves when their cultures are integrated into the learning environment.

Throughout this book, I argue that any educator who seeks to develop an understanding of students' cultures automatically places themselves in the best

---

[1] Howard, T. (2020). *Why race and culture matter in schools: Closing the achievement gap in America's classrooms* (2nd ed.). Teachers College Press.
[2] Saifer, S., Edwards, K., Ellis, D., Ko, L., & Stuczynski, A. (2011). *Culturally responsive standards-based teaching: Classroom to community and back.* Corwin.
[3] Ibid.

position to elevate student achievement. In fact, I believe understanding students' cultures is the most necessary step to engaging students in culturally responsive instruction. If we are going to embrace the "whole child," we cannot expect students to leave their cultures at home in order to succeed in the learning environment. Therefore, it is the responsibility of educators to address cultural misconceptions that might be embedded in our beliefs on an implicit level.

Misconceptions about Culture

Over the years of coaching educators, I have noticed two major misconceptions that educators often embrace about culture: Culture is static and unchanging, and the terms, Culture and Race are synonymous. If unaddressed, these misconceptions will prohibit educators from effectively engaging students in culturally responsive teaching and learning.

Misconception #1 - Culture is static and unchanging.

Too often, educators cling to a narrow view of culture that fails to take into consideration the complexities of culture. Culture is not static and unchanging! It is rather nuanced, fluid, dynamic, and ever-changing. When we embrace the misconception that culture is static and unchanging, we are likely to think that students of today automatically identify with the cultural ways of the past. This is not true. For example, teenagers who identify with Hip-Hop culture in 2023 do not share the same values, norms, language, attitudes, beliefs, customs, and habits as young people who identified with Hip-Hop culture during the late 1980s. This is why many parents who grew up listening to Big Daddy Kane, KRS 1, LL Cool J, Queen Latifah, MC Lyte, and Grandmaster Flash & The Furious Five struggle to understand the Hip-Hop music their children are infatuated with in today's time. While each group still may identify with the Hip-Hop cultural identity, they both must recognize that the identity of Hip-Hop culture has changed. Overall, culture is not static and unchanging because culture is dynamic, nuanced, and ever-evolving.

Misconception #2 – Culture and Race are synonymous.

The second and most popular misconception is the notion that culture and race mean the exact same thing. This is simply not true. When culture is equated to race, people who identify with a particular racial group may develop a false sense of confidence in their ability to effectively teach students who look like them. For example, a White teacher is not automatically going to experience success when teaching White students. Racial identity is not a pedagogical skill. There are countless White teachers working in predominantly White schools that will not have their teaching contracts renewed due to poor performance. Similarly, being Black does not automatically qualify Black educators to successfully engage Black students in culturally responsive teaching. Black culture is not a monolith. It encompasses the cultural heritage of individuals from across the African diaspora on continents such as South America, North America, Africa, and many other places where Black people reside. The point of the matter is culture goes beyond racial classifications.

    When we conflate race and culture, we fail to realize that individuals can share the same racial identity and yet ideologically reside on different ends of the cultural spectrum. For example, a Black male student who grew up on the east side of Chicago may embrace a cultural identity that is easily distinguished from a Black male student whose family emigrated to the United States from Haiti. While the two students may share the same phenotypical features (i.e., melanated skin) and racial identity, they may not share the same cultural beliefs, values, and ways of being. The same is true for a White female student from Des Moines, Iowa, and a White female student from Moscow, Russia. The two students may share the same racial identity, but they may not share the same language, customs, interests, or worldview. This popular misconception must be eschewed if we are seeking to become culturally responsive educators. When educators lump all students of the same racial identity into the same "cultural category," we are likely to engage in culturally responsive malpractice driven by stereotypical racial assumptions. This is not what it means to be culturally responsive.

Nevertheless, by identifying misconceptions about culture, we place ourselves in the best position to build on a solid foundation. So, let us begin our journey toward becoming culturally responsive educators!

BECOMING CULTURALLY RESPONSIVE EDUCATORS

5 Necessary Action Steps

Table of Contents

Prelude - Clarifying Culture 6

Introduction: Inspiration to Become Culturally Responsive Educators 16

Section 1: Culturally Responsive Educators (CRE) 26

Section 2: Five Necessary Action Steps 66

Step 1 - Develop Historical Awareness 68

Step 2 - Foster Multicultural Consciousness 94

Step 3 - Apply Culturally Responsive Approaches 120

Step 4 - Prioritize Family and Community Engagement 154

Step 5 - Advocate for Culturally Responsive Schools 173

Section 3: Confidence and Culturally Responsive Self-Efficacy 189

Conclusion - Committing to the Process of Becoming Culturally Responsive Educators 198

Meet the Author 206

Downloadable Images, Diagrams, and Frameworks 209

Introduction: Inspiration to Become Culturally Responsive Educators

"Caring teachers honor differences of and among students."
- GENEVA GAY

"Every child deserves a champion: an adult who will never give up on them, who understands the power of connection and insists they become the best they can possibly be."
- RITA PIERSON

While working as the Title 1 Instructional Coach at one of the largest Title 1 middle schools in Virginia, I was immersed in the exhaustive work and world of teaching, like many educators within this profession. I would often stay up late reviewing pacing guides and curriculum frameworks. I also evaluated countless lesson plans from teachers, conducted observations of their classroom teaching practices, and engaged them in coaching cycles to build their instructional capacity. Additionally, I led professional development for the entire school.

We Are Inspired by Students

Over 80% of the students at my school identified as African American, Hispanic, or bi-racial. In addition, almost 100% of the students were eligible for free or reduced meals. If the analogy of track and field could be used to describe the pace of day-to-day life within my school, I would have to say every day was a 100-meter dash. Every educator knew that once they entered the building, they had to be prepared for a full sprint for eight consecutive hours. While we worked diligently to increase the academic achievement of our students, we often failed to consider the role that students' cultures played in the learning environment. Yet, one student shifted my entire paradigm for teaching and learning during a classroom observation of a 7th-grade science teacher who was teaching a lesson on genetics featuring James Watson and Francis Crick.

    While I was surveying the class and jotting down notes about the percentage of students who were fully engaged during the lesson, I noticed one student staring at me. His name was Carlos, and he was Hispanic. Carlos and I had a great rapport. He often would find me on the bus ramp during the afternoon dismissal to chat about sports-related news. I would also rely on Carlos to help me translate for and assist emerging English language learners because he was fluent in English and Spanish. Yet, on this particular day, Carlos was not paying any attention to the teacher. He was simply staring at me as I looked around, occasionally jotting down anecdotal notes.

    When the class period ended, all of the students anxiously headed toward the cafeteria for lunch. I accompanied the students because I was responsible for serving as one of the cafeteria monitors. While I was walking down the hallway, Carlos approached me with a serious and concerned expression on his face and said, "Mr. Taylor, are there any Hispanic scientists?" To be honest, I was caught off guard by this question, but I immediately responded, "Absolutely!" Carlos then inquired further, "Then why don't we learn about them?" It was at that moment that the proverbial light bulb went off in my mind. I began to think about cultural representation in the curriculum, the role that culture plays in teaching and learning, and the number of students who probably felt just like Carlos.

      The question Carlos asked me resonated deeply within me. It challenged my pedagogy, made me conscious of the lack of diversity across the curriculum, and made me consider how students may feel when their culture is not centered in the instructional setting. Carlos served as a much-needed inspiration for me. He had an authentic and genuine desire to see his culture reflected in the academic space. I will never forget that moment in my career. It served as a major catalyst for me on my educational journey to become culturally responsive. In addition, it inspired me to complete my dissertation on "*The*

Relationship Between Multicultural Consciousness and Culturally Responsive Teaching Self-Efficacy."[4]

We are Inspired by Educators

In addition to being inspired by students, most educators have been inspired by other educators. Many of us can look back over our lives and identify those "Teachers with a Purpose" who have inspired us to become educators. These professionals include paraeducators, librarians, counselors, bus drivers, teachers, and leaders who have helped us develop self-confidence. During my K-12 experience, I only had two educators who I would consider unforgettable: Mr. Jobie Boone (4th grade) and Mrs. Patricia Bookman (High School English). I have written extensively about these two individuals in almost every book I have published. I also publicly thanked them on the dedication page of my dissertation. I have always been determined to give them their proverbial "flowers" because the impact they made on my life was just that massive. I know, without a doubt, I would not be who I am today without their influence. I

---

[4] Taylor, J. H. (2022). *Relationship between multicultural consciousness and culturally responsive teaching self-efficacy* (Publication No. 30241427) [Doctoral disseration, Regent University]. ProQuest Dissertations & Theses Global.

certainly would not have gone to college or pursued advanced degrees had they not been my teachers.

I can honestly say these educators genuinely cared about me. They served as inspiration during a time in my life when I did not feel safe and secure in school. They were culturally responsive educators indeed. Mr. Boone, the only African American male educator I ever had during my K-12 experience, had a way of connecting with his students and communicating high expectations. He was firm, fair, and determined to make us rise to his elevated expectations. Mrs. Bookman, a middle-aged White woman who wore eccentric colors and was nicknamed "Mrs. Frizzle" by her students, was determined to spark students' interest in literacy. I will never forget the day she challenged us to write a brief biography about an author of our choice. She distributed a list of authors, including Henry David Thoreau, William Shakespeare, Mark Twain, Langston Hughes, and a plethora of other notable authors. She explained that we could only choose one author from the list to write about. Immediately upon looking at the list, I was discouraged. I was not interested in any of those individuals.

At that point in my life, I was infatuated with Nasir Jones (affectionately known as Nas). Nas is a Hip-Hop legend who most consider a "God-Emcee." That means he's on another level when compared to other rappers. In my opinion, he was and continues to be the greatest rapper in the universe. During my time in high school, he wrote some of the most creative Hip-Hop lyrics I had ever heard, and I wanted to write about him. So, at the end of that class period, I lingered a little longer in an attempt to speak with Mrs. Bookman when no other students were around. I approached her desk and said, "Hey, Mrs. Bookman! To be honest, I don't want to do a biography about any of those guys. I want to write about Nasir Jones." Mrs. Bookman responded with a concerned facial expression, "I've never heard about Nasir Jones." I quickly said, "Great. Once I finish with this paper, you will know everything about Nasir Jones." She said, "Ok, I look forward to learning about him." I rushed home that day, eager to get started with my biography. Up to that point in my life, I had never been more passionate about writing, or any academic endeavor for that matter. I had always been a struggling student in high school. During my freshman year, I skipped 14 days of school and had a cumulative grade point average of 0.75. I was certainly heading down the wrong path.

  Yet, Mrs. Bookman was integral in helping me find my focus. She modeled for me what culturally responsive teaching is all about. She centered learning experiences around my interests and infused the things that I was passionate about into the curriculum. This is exactly what culturally responsive educators seek to do daily. Nevertheless, after I completed the assignment, I had to present my work to the class. Since I embraced my individuality wholeheartedly, I did not write a traditional essay. I wrote my biography in a rhyme scheme. I was attempting to channel my "inner Nas." After I read my work aloud, the class erupted in celebration with shouts of, "That was fire," "Pure dopeness," and "He got bars!" I had never been affirmed in the academic space by my peers until that day, which was literally magical for me.

    I share this story because many educators struggle to help students make "magic" in the classroom, particularly African American and other minoritized students. However, I want every educator to know that you can reach the students you teach. Your race and culture are not barriers to your ability to help students achieve at the highest levels. Mrs. Bookman was a middle-aged White woman. However, she cared deeply about the students she taught and was willing to do whatever it would take to reach us. She embodied the mindset of a culturally responsive educator by allowing me to bring my Hip-Hop culture into the classroom. Through this book, I seek to inspire educators to utilize the integration of students' cultures as instructional tools. Similar to how Mrs. Bookman empowered me to write by affirming the brilliance of Hip-Hop authors, I encourage educators to empower students through their students' cultural lenses. No student should feel as if he or she must leave their culture at home to succeed in school.

Structure of this Book

This book contains practical stories from my K-12 experience as a Special Education teacher, Title 1 Instructional Coach, and full-time Educational Consultant. It also highlights some of the latest research on the topic of culturally responsive teaching. In addition, I have created frameworks and diagrams to help make abstract concepts visible and easier to digest. Through this book, my goal is to help you commit to the process of becoming culturally responsive educators who empower young people to reveal their brilliance to the world.

This book is structured in three sections. The first section provides a review of literature pertaining to *culturally responsive educators*, why this language was preferred over culturally responsive teachers, and an explanation of what these educators do differently when compared to traditional educators. The second section is the lengthiest section because it highlights and explains the five necessary action steps educators must take if they desire to become culturally responsive educators. Each of the five steps contains a review of existing literature, diagrams, and templates designed to help readers better understand how to engage in each step. In addition, the steps conclude with an overview and extension questions to help the reader engage in self-reflection.

The last section focuses on the collective role and responsibility that each educator must embrace. It is not sufficient for children to have access to only one or two culturally responsive educators. I argue that students need a culturally responsive school experience, which means every educator must take accountability for helping to develop and support other educators on their journey to become culturally responsive as well. The conclusion of the book challenges educators to commit to the process of becoming culturally responsive educators by employing the five necessary action steps. The key takeaway is, "No one ever arrives as a culturally responsive educator. We all remain in a constant state of perpetually becoming culturally responsive educators." Let the journey begin! #OnPurpose

Section 1: Culturally Responsive Educators (CRE)

"There are different attitudes in different cultural groups about which characteristics make for a good teacher. Thus, it is impossible to create a model for the good teacher without taking issues of culture and community context into account."
- LISA DELPIT[5]

Essential Question: What is a "Culturally Responsive Educator?"

The need for culturally responsive educators (CRE) has never been greater. Educators in the current American public school system are expected to successfully teach the most culturally diverse student body in our nation's history. Students of color now comprise the majority of students enrolled in the public school system (De Brey et al., 2021).[6] Yet, the majority of educators across the United States identify racially as White (De Brey et al., 2021). Consequently, students of color are likely to be taught by teachers who do not share a common racial or cultural background, nor do they share similar lived

---

[5] Delpit, L. (2006). *Other people's children: Cultural conflict in the classroom.* The New Press.
[6] De Brey, C., Snyder, T. D., Zhang, A., & Dillow, S. A. (2021). *Digest of education statistics 2019 (NCES 2021-009).* National Center for Education Statistics, Institute of Education Sciences. U.S. Department of Education.

experiences (Siwatu et al., 2016).[7] Cultural differences between teachers and students are not necessarily a deal breaker if the educator is culturally responsive, but research has documented issues that arise when teachers lack the ability to respond to cultural diversity appropriately.

According to Bonner et al. (2017), cultural differences between teachers and students can lead to academic and behavioral challenges if teachers are not equipped to engage diverse learners in the teaching and learning process.[8] This reality calls for a new paradigm in teacher preparation designed to help teachers develop attitudes, beliefs, and dispositions that will enable them to meet the unique needs of culturally diverse learners. To ensure educators are equipped with the mindset and pedagogical posture needed to effectively engage an increasingly diverse student population, educator training and preparation must empower educators while increasing their efficacy in teaching culturally diverse learners (Gay, 2018).[9] In other words, every educator must strive to

---

[7] Siwatu, K. O., Chesnut, S. R., Alejandro, A. Y., & Young, H. A. (2016). Examining preservice teachers' culturally responsive teaching self-efficacy doubts. *The Teacher Educator, 51*(4), 277-296. https://doi.org/10.1080/08878730.2016.1192709

[8] Bonner, P. J., Warren, S. R., & Jiang, Y. H. (2017). Voices from urban classrooms: Teachers' perceptions on instructing diverse students and using culturally responsive teaching. *Education and Urban Society, 50* (8), 697-726. http://dx.doi.org/10.1177/0013124517713820

[9] Gay, G. (2018). *Culturally responsive teaching: Theory, research, and practice* (3rd ed.). Teachers College Press.

become a "culturally responsive educator" (Irvine & Armento, 2001, p. 23).[10]

Preferred Language - CRE

While the term "culturally responsive teacher" (CRT) is more popular in the research literature, I use the term culturally responsive educator (CRE) to be more inclusive of educators who may not align with the traditional role of a teacher (i.e., principals, guidance counselors, academic coaches, dean of students, office staff, etc.). A CRE is an educator who employs culturally responsive approaches and a variety of instructional practices to meet the unique needs of culturally diverse students. A CRE rejects deficit narratives about students' cultures and chooses to view students' cultures as assets in the learning environment (Taylor, 2022).[11] I argue that CREs understand that knowledge of a student's culture is the most effective instructional tool an educator can possess in the learning environment.

According to Dr. Geneva Gay (2018), a CRE uses the "cultural knowledge, prior experiences, frames of reference, and performance styles of ethnically diverse

---

[10] Irvine, J. J. & Armento, B. J. (2001). *Culturally responsive teaching: Lesson planning for elementary and middle grades.* McGraw-Hill.
[11] Taylor, J. H. (2022). Relationship between multicultural consciousness and culturally responsive teaching self-efficacy. *Journal for Multicultural Education, 17*(1), 31-42. https://doi.org/10.1108/JME-01-2022-0006

students to make learning encounters more relevant to and effective for them."[12] Hammond (2015) alluded to the notion that CREs have high expectations for students and seek to build students' intellectual capacities by focusing on information processing.[13] In other words, CREs provide students with rigorous learning experiences, hold students to high academic expectations, and take ownership of student achievement. These instructional actions flow from the belief that each child possesses inherent brilliance and untapped potential. Very much in alignment with the work of Dr. Gholdy Muhammad, CREs are the type of educators who see their work as a mission to "cultivate genius."[14] Therefore, CREs teach with a higher purpose (calling) in mind. They use rigorous instruction to build students' cognitive abilities as a means to equip students with the tools they will need to radically change their worlds for the better.[15] Thus, one goal of CREs is to move students from dependent learners to independent learners capable of taking on any challenge in and out of school (Hammond, 2015).

---

[12] Ibid., p. 36.
[13] Hammond, Z. L. (2015). *Culturally responsive teaching and the brain: Promoting authentic engagement and rigor among culturally and linguistically diverse students*. Corwin.
[14] Muhammad, G. E. (2020). *Cultivating genius*. Scholastic Teaching Resources.
[15] Hammond, Z. L. (2015). *Culturally responsive teaching and the brain: Promoting authentic engagement and rigor among culturally and linguistically diverse students*. Corwin.

I believe it is of the utmost importance to emphasize that CREs are not on a mission to "fix" children. Children do not need to be fixed. Rather, adults' perceptions about children and their potential need to be fixed. As Zaretta Hammond (2015) articulated, "Culturally responsive teaching isn't a set of engagement strategies you use on students. Instead, think of it as a mindset, a way of looking at the world" (p. 52).[16] A CRE is committed to perpetual personal growth to help students achieve at the highest levels possible.

What Do Culturally Responsive Educators Do?

First things first, CREs *prioritize relationships with students*. Since the goal is to be more responsive to students, one must commit to learning about students. How can educators be responsive to a culture they refuse to understand? How can educators respond appropriately to something they do not possess knowledge of? Therefore, CREs use the rapport building process to gain meaningful knowledge about students' interests, aspirations, and lived experiences in order to design learning experiences that students will gravitate to and

---

[16] Hammond, Z. L. (2015). *Culturally responsive teaching and the brain: Promoting authentic engagement and rigor among culturally and linguistically diverse students.* Corwin.

connect with. Taylor (2018) asserted that CREs practice "Relational Teaching."[17]

According to Taylor (2018), relational teaching is a teaching methodology determined to "create an atmosphere of love in the learning environment where every student feels capable, connected, and cared for."[18] Expounding on the connection between caring and culturally responsive practices, Dr. Geneva Gay (2000) explained, "Caring is one of the major pillars of culturally responsive pedagogy for ethnically diverse students. It is manifested in the form of teacher attitudes, expectations, and behaviors about students' human value, intellectual capability, and performance responsibilities" (p. 45).[19] One cannot be culturally responsive without a commitment to building caring relationships with students. Caring relationships allow students to feel a sense of security in the school environment. If students feel insecure, they will be less likely to share information about their lives outside of school, which requires a level of vulnerability. Therefore, the relationship building process is at the foundation of all culturally responsive practices. It allows educators to learn about differences in students' communication and learning

---

[17] Taylor, J. H. (2018) *Relational teaching: Connection is the key*. Kindle Direct Publishing.
[18] Ibid., p. 34.
[19] Gay, G. (2018). *Culturally responsive teaching: Theory, research and practice.* Teachers College Press.

styles, which is essential knowledge teachers must possess.[20]

Additionally, CREs seek to understand the nuances of students' cultures and the unique realities confronting them. Yet, obtaining cultural knowledge is not an easy task. In some cases, this knowledge must be obtained indirectly from students. For example, it may not be wise for an educator to approach a 2nd grader and say, "Tell me about your culture." Clearly, that may be an inappropriate and ineffective technique for learning about that particular student's culture. However, this approach may be more fruitful with a high school student who is aware of his or her culture and has the ability to clearly articulate oneself. Nevertheless, educators who desire to become CREs must be empathic enough to connect with diverse students, motivated enough to commit to life-long professional growth, and instructionally savvy enough to employ the right strategy or practice to meet the unique academic needs of diverse learners. This means educators seeking to become CREs must be willing to roll up their sleeves and commit to the process of learning about students' cultures. Therefore, prioritizing the relationship building process with students is so critical. It is through the development of meaningful relationships with students

---

[20] Ibid.

that cultural knowledge is authentically and organically exchanged.

So, here are 3 concrete and foundational actions that will define CREs. CREs: 1) Prioritize building meaningful relationships with students, 2) diversify their knowledge base, which increases their cultural competence, and 3) believe in students' brilliance by embracing high expectations.

#1 - Prioritize Building Meaningful Relationships

Since every child is different, educators will most likely need to employ different strategies to facilitate the relationship-building process. For example, for some of my students, I have used student interest surveys, questionnaires, or one-on-one interviews to facilitate the relationship-building process that will lead to an exchange of cultural information. I have also used "2 by 10 chats" and "Get to Know Me" activities to facilitate authentic exchanges of cultural information. At other times, I have used journal prompts or simply asked questions to spark a conversation that will lead to the exchange of information.

Here are a few examples of questions that can lead to an exchange of cultural information: What is your favorite food? Who is your favorite musician, songwriter, or performer? What do you usually do when you leave school? What do you normally do during the summer break or during the winter break? What is your favorite game to play? Sometimes, students respond to questions similar to the ones listed above and share information that provides great insight into their cultural backgrounds and lived experiences. When educators create a space where students feel comfortable enough to freely share insights about their worlds, educators can gain a wealth of cultural knowledge about students.

> **PURPOSE**
>
> Culturally responsive educators prioritize relationships with students.
> - Dr. Jahkari Taylor

So, I certainly encourage educators to employ numerous techniques to intentionally build relationships with students. I want to emphasize the need to be intentional and strategic when selecting resources and activities for building relationships with culturally diverse students. Do not simply download a worksheet from a popularized teacher resource website without analyzing its utility in your context. Always remember, a one-size fits all approach to teaching and learning is not a research-based best practice to meet the needs of culturally diverse students. Developing a caring relationship with students also looks like properly vetting resources prior to employing them in the classroom. Any time resources are not properly vetted, educators run the risk of causing psychological or emotional harm to diverse students.

For example, CBS New York (2018) reported that a middle school teacher in the Bronx, New York, "told several Black children to lie on the floor during a lesson about the slave trade and the cruel conditions aboard slave ships" (p.1).[21] When one of the students laughed at the teacher, the teacher allegedly stepped on the child's back and said, "See how it feels to be a slave." Now, clearly, this is an extreme situation, but it shows us how problematic it can be for students when educators fail to prioritize caring relationships or vet lesson plans to ensure they will not lead to psychological, emotional, and physical harm.

Avoiding Culturally Destructive Practices

Educators who develop caring relationships with their students will be less likely to engage in culturally destructive practices. Culturally destructive practices refer to any practices that harm students. These practices do not have to be as extreme as the one mentioned in the last paragraph, where a student is physically harmed. Instead, it can look like a microaggressive comment where a

---

[21] CBS New York. (2018 February 2). *Bronx middle school teacher accused of stepping on student during slavery lesson.* https://www.cbsnews.com/amp/newyork/news/slavery-lesson-outrage

student is left feeling belittled or undervalued. For example, when White educators tell Black students, "I don't see color when I look at you," students are often left feeling as if their racial/ethnic experiences are not real. This can be psychologically and emotionally damaging to students who require a safe space to thrive academically. In addition, culturally destructive practices may manifest when an educator fails to acknowledge a student's culture. When a student's culture is not acknowledged as an asset in the educational space, an implicit message is sent informing the child that his or her culture is not welcomed or valued in this space. Regardless of how or to what extent culturally destructive practices manifest in the educational space, we must understand that they are harmful and serve as a barrier to the relationship-building process. Therefore, they have no place in schools.

#2 - Diversify One's Knowledge Base

Not only do CREs prioritize relationships with students and authentically get to know students to reduce the occurrence of culturally destructive practices, but the second thing CREs do is seek to *diversify their knowledge base*. Diversifying one's knowledge base refers to the intentional process of exposing oneself to the genius of diverse cultures and their contributions to the world. By familiarizing themselves with cultural diversity, CREs will be able to understand and appreciate cultural differences. This knowledge is necessary to respond appropriately to cultural diversity within the classroom. In the research literature, this is also referred to as "cultural competence."

The Necessity of Cultural Competence

According to the National Education Association (NEA) (2015), cultural competence refers to "the ability to successfully teach students who come from cultures other than our own. It entails developing certain personal and interpersonal awareness and sensitivities, developing certain bodies of cultural knowledge, and mastering a set of skills that, taken together, underlie effective cross-cultural teaching" (p. 1).[22] Possessing cultural competence is key to becoming a CRE. Educators can begin the process of increasing their cultural competence by prioritizing relationships with students and intentionally diversifying their knowledge base. So, you might be wondering, "Where do I begin the process of diversifying my knowledge base?" I believe the first step is listening with the intention of raising your awareness of diverse perspectives.

There are a plethora of podcasts, YouTube channels, and documentaries where diverse individuals

---

[22] National Education Association [NEA]. (2015). *Diversity toolkit: Cultural competence for educators.* http://www.nea.org/tools/30402.htm.

share their lived experiences. By simply lending your ear to listen, you will be exposed to perspectives that are quite different from yours. For example, I have had many discussions with Black and White educational leaders who grew up in a middle-class, two-parent home. Their upbringing and lived experiences were very different than mine as a Black male who grew up in an impoverished single-parent home. Through those conversations, we all realized that we have to challenge assumptions that are often associated with how we grew up. However, if we were unwilling to listen with the intent to understand, we would not have been able to learn about each other's lived experiences, customs, norms, and values.

Along with podcasts, there are thousands of books written by diverse authors that can help you diversify your knowledge base. Educators can also read biographical literature about culturally diverse individuals to capture a more accurate understanding of diversity, as opposed to being informed by media messages which often have slanted or biased renditions of cultural diversity. The unfortunate truth is most educators (and their students) lack exposure to books, movies, and other creative works designed by diverse authors.

We can quickly assess the extent to which we have been exposed to a diversified knowledge base by asking ourselves the following questions: How many books have I read that were written by diverse authors? In order to diversify our knowledge base, we must actively and intentionally seek out learning materials that will increase our cultural competence.

> **PURPOSE PUSHERS**
>
> Culturally responsive educators seek to diversify their knowledge base.
> - Dr. Jahkari Taylor

10 Books to Help Educators Diversify Their Knowledge Base

Here is a list of books written by diverse authors that can help educators diversify their knowledge base and increase cultural competence:

1. *Why Are All the Black Kids Sitting Together in the Cafeteria?: And Other Conversations About Race* - Beverly Daniel Tatum
2. *To Selena, With Love* - Chris Perez
3. *School Clothes: A Collective Memoir of Black Student Witness* - Jarvis R. Givens

4. *We Want to Do More Than Survive: Abolitionist Teaching and the Pursuit of Educational Freedom* - Bettina Love
5. *My Beloved World* - Sonia Sotomayor
6. *The DreamKeepers: Successful Teachers of African American Children* - Gloria Ladson-Billings
7. *We Can't Teach What We Don't Know: White Teachers, Multiracial Schools* - Gary R. Howard
8. *Cultivating Genius: An Equity Framework for Culturally and Historically Responsive Literacy* - Gholdy Muhammad
9. *Culturally Responsive Teaching & The Brain: Promoting Authentic Engagement and Rigor Among Culturally and Linguistically Diverse Students* - Zaretta Hammond
10. *For White Folks Who Teach in the Hood… And the Rest of Y'all Too: Reality Pedagogy and Urban Education (Race, Education, and Democracy)* - Christopher Emdin

Become a Student of Your Students

We also must be ready and willing to learn from the students in our context. Sometimes, students can teach us more about their culture than any podcast, book, or documentary. Again, this is why the relationship building process is essential. Abacioglu et al. (2020) emphasized the notion that teachers can build a culturally responsive knowledge base by establishing meaningful relationships with students. These relationships can inform educators' understanding of students' cultural values, traditions, languages, and identities.[23]

#3 - Believe in Students' Brilliance

Lastly, and most importantly, CRE must *believe in the inherent brilliance of culturally diverse youth*. Beliefs matter in education! This point cannot be emphasized enough. Brown (2007) wrote, "One of the most important aspects of a culturally responsive classroom is the teacher's belief that students from culturally and linguistically diverse (CLD) backgrounds want to learn" (p. 60). Howard (2020) stated, "The belief that all students are capable of learning is essential to culturally responsive teaching" (p. 77).[24] Furthermore, Gay (2018) stated, "Culturally responsive teachers have unequivocal faith in the human dignity and intellectual capabilities of their students" (p. 52).[25] In other words, they believe in the inherent brilliance of culturally diverse students. CREs work to develop students' critical thinking skills. Their goal

---

[23] Abacioglu, C. S., Volman, M., & Fischer, A. H. (2020). Teachers' multicultural attitudes and perspective-taking abilities as factors in culturally responsive teaching. *British Journal of Educational Psychology, 90,* 736-752. https://doi.org/10.1111/bjep.12328
[24] Howard, T. (2020). *Why race and culture matter in schools.* Teachers College Press.
[25] Gay, G. (2018). *Culturally responsive teaching: Theory, research, and practice.*

is to raise students' higher level thinking skills and equip them with an ability to solve complex issues confronting their communities. Dr. Gloria Ladson-Billings refers to this development as "critical consciousness."[26]

Tapping into Students' Brilliance

Educators can help students develop critical consciousness by showing them how academic skills can be applied to help themselves and their communities. For example, when I was a high school special education teacher, I required my students to engage in "Daily Journal Prompts" at the start of each day. I purchased journals for each of my students and asked them to write a minimum of 10 sentences for each entry. Most of the journal entries focused on socioemotional concepts because my students were found eligible for special education services under the *IDEA* category of Emotional Disability. I often explained that writing was not just an "academic skill" needed in school but rather an essential skill necessary for life outside of school. Since many of my students struggled to manage their emotions, I helped them to see writing as a coping strategy for processing their feelings. The journal prompts often challenged them to reflect on moments of frustration, fear, sadness, loneliness, joy, and many other

---

[26] Ladson-Billings, G. (1995a). But that's just good teaching! The case for culturally relevant pedagogy. *Theory into Practice, 34*(3), 159-165. https://doi.org/10.1080/00405849509543675

emotions. Then, I would ask them to express themselves through their responses.

At the beginning of the year, most of my students were hesitant to demonstrate vulnerability in their journals. I believe this was the case because we were still establishing a positive rapport as a class, plus students had never viewed writing in such a practical way. They only viewed writing through the lens of an assignment reserved for a traditional Language Arts activity. Meaning, they viewed it as merely an academic exercise and not relevant to their realities. Yet, once they became familiar with writing as a practical tool to help them manage their own emotions, I started to introduce writing as a tool to address issues in their communities. Also, although not required, some students would feel inspired enough to share their journal entries with the class.

Additionally, on occasion, I would pair students or assign them to a small group of three to five students within the classroom. I would provide them with a rubric detailing the expectations and requirements, and I would ask them to collaborate to create a plan to solve an issue within their community. On one occasion, students created a plan to clean up and beautify a local park in their community. They felt that the city was committed to every park except the park in their community, which was located in the poorest borough of the city. Therefore, they created a proposal detailing what they would need to execute what they called, "The Big Pick Up." Their goal was to raise money and purchase mulch, gloves, and trash bags in an attempt to restore the park so younger children would have a safe and sanitary place to play. Not only did my students write a proposal, create a name for their project, and map out the step-by-step logistics, these young people executed at the highest level. They even created flyers and posted them around the school, soliciting volunteers to assist with their project. Teachers donated money, supplies, snacks, and beverages to support the students. Once they acquired the resources they needed, they were empowered and filled with excitement and pride to reinvest in their own community.

       This is just a small example of how CREs can provide students with opportunities to employ academic skills to address issues in their community. Remember, CREs seek to integrate students' cultures, lived experiences, interests, and aspirations into the teaching and learning process. If we are willing to guide and empower young people to address issues in their communities, they are more than brilliant enough to use these academic skills to bring real solutions to their own communities.

Do We Really Believe in Students' Brilliance?

If we were to ask every educator in K-12 classrooms across the United States if they believed in the inherent brilliance of each student, I am not too sure that 100% of the educators would declare, "I believe all children are brilliant." While I do believe most educators would affirm that declaration, I am persuaded that children deserve more than "most." Students need 100% of their educators to believe in their potential. Within our educational system, we are not there yet, which is why we need every educator to become a CRE.

> **PURPOSE PUSHERS**
>
> Culturally responsive educators believe in the inherent brilliance of culturally diverse youth.
> - Dr. Jahkari Taylor

Deficit Thinking and Implicit Biases

In every school, there are pockets of educators who honestly believe culturally and linguistically diverse youth are not brilliant. These are the educators who believe diverse youth lack the capacity to learn at a high level. This type of thinking is referred to as "deficit thinking" in the research literature. Deficit thinking refers to implicit or explicit negative attitudes and beliefs about students.[27] This type of thinking is usually fueled and maintained by individuals who have not yet identified their implicit biases about students of color, their families, and their communities. According to Hammond (2015), "implicit bias refers to the unconscious attitudes and stereotypes that shape our responses to certain groups. Implicit bias operates involuntarily, often without one's awareness or intentional control, which is different from explicit racism" (p. 29).[28] Also, Patton Davis and Museus (2019) noted, "deficit thinking holds students from historically oppressed populations responsible for the challenges and inequalities that they face" (p. 119).[29] Deficit thinking leads educators to blame school failure of students of color on "the students' lack of readiness to learn in the classroom, the parents' lack of interest in their education, and the families' overall lifestyle" (Walker, 2011, p. 577).[30]

Rather than focusing on educator attitudes, historical inequities, and the systemic influences that

---

[27] Patton Davis, L., & Museus, S. (2019). What is deficit thinking? An analysis of conceptualizations of deficit thinking and implications for scholarly research. *Currents, 1*(1), 117-130. http://dx.doi.org/10.3998/currents.17387731.0001.110

[28] Hammond, Z. L. (2015). *Culturally responsive teaching and the brain: Promoting authentic engagement and rigor among culturally and linguistically diverse students.* Corwin.

[29] Patton Davis, L., & Museus, S. (2019). What is deficit thinking? *Currents, 1*(1). http://dx.doi.org/10.3998/currents.17387731.0001.110

[30] Walker, K. L. (Haynes). (2011). Deficit thinking and the effective teacher. *Education and Urban Society, 43*(5), 576–597. https://doi.org/10.1177/0013124510380721

shape disparities in social and educational outcomes, deficit thinking "situates school failure in the minds, bodies, communities, and culture of students" (Dudley-Marling, 2015, p. 1).[31] Dudley-Marling (2015) explained that deficit thinking dominates schooling practices in the United States and Canada. Educators who maintain negative attitudes rooted in deficit thinking about culturally diverse students will not only be challenged to effectively teach students of color, but they also will contribute to and sustain educational inequities. For these reasons, becoming a CRE is essential if educators do not want to perpetuate inequities.

Why Does Every School Need Culturally Responsive Educators?

CREs are needed in every school to reduce the educational inequities associated with cultural misunderstandings and a general lack of cultural competence.

Special Education Needs CREs

Not only are CREs needed in the general education setting working with students without disabilities, but CREs

---

[31] Dudley-Marling, C. (2015). The resilience of deficit thinking. *Journal of Teaching and Learning, 10*(1), p.1-12. https://doi.org/10.22329/jtl.v10i1.4171

are also essential in the inclusion and self-contained settings working with students with disabilities. When it comes to the lack of academic progress of students with disabilities, Chu (2016) noted that deficit thinking hinders the academic and behavioral outcomes of culturally diverse students in the general education setting as well as the special education setting.[32] Chu (2016) also found that deficit-thinking paradigms in special education practices led to students not receiving appropriate special education services. To counter negative attitudes associated with deficit thinking, Chu (2016) recommended that special education teachers "focus on utilizing culturally- and linguistically-appropriate and relevant practices" (p. 42).[33] The need for CREs in special education is not only validated in the research literature, but I have witnessed this need while working in the context of K-12 public schools.

When I was a Title 1 Instructional Coach, I was tasked with coaching 12 science teachers and 20 special education teachers. One day, I entered an inclusion class during preservice week to check in with a few educators.

---

[32] Chu, S. (2016). Developing a scale to investigate in-service special education teacher efficacy for serving students from culturally and linguistically diverse backgrounds. *Journal of Curriculum and Teaching* 5(1), 39-51. http://dx.doi.org/10.5430/jct.v5n1p39

[33] Chu, S. (2016). Developing a scale to investigate in-service special education teacher efficacy for serving students from culturally and linguistically diverse backgrounds. *Journal of Curriculum and Teaching* 5 (1), 39-51. http://dx.doi.org/10.5430/jct.v5n1p39

My goal was to see how I might be of service to them during that particular academic year. Upon entering the classroom, I enthusiastically greeted two educators by saying, "What's going on? Are y'all ready for a great year?" One teacher responded and said, "Absolutely, but I'm a little concerned about what my test scores may look like this year." She was referring to the standardized state-sanctioned end-of-course assessments. I said, "What do you mean?" She continued, "I think the best I'll be able to do is around 69% because I have 26 students, 8 of which have IEPs." As a former special education teacher, I was confused and caught off guard. With a befuddled expression on my face, I responded, "Are you counting students with disabilities as an automatic failure on your end-of-course assessments before you teach them?" Stunned by my response, the educator quickly tried to retract her statement by saying that was not what she meant. She explained that, based on her teaching experiences, she had never witnessed students with disabilities passing the end-of-course assessments. She could see I was in total disbelief.

    That day taught me a valuable lesson about how educators' attitudes and beliefs impact their approaches to engaging students in the teaching and learning process. Now, when I see patterns of student underperformance, I often think about how those students are perceived by their teachers. I think to myself: What role might deficit thinking play in the academic performance of those students? Are those students being hindered by the attitudes, beliefs, and dispositions of their educators?

My experiences lead me to process in this manner because I know some students are not afforded access to rigorous learning assignments because teachers believe they are "too low" and "unable to handle rigorous assignments." Therefore, these students are robbed of opportunities to demonstrate their unique brilliance. I strongly believe this type of deficit thinking contributes to the chronic underperformance of many diverse students, including students with disabilities.

General Education Needs CREs

In another study, Keefer (2017) utilized a case study methodology to explore the presence of deficit thinking among five social studies educators in Florida.[34] It is noteworthy to mention that the teachers were diverse. Of the five educators, one was a Latina teacher who worked at an urban Title 1 school, two were White females who worked at a non-Title 1 suburban school, one was a Black male who taught at an affluent urban school, and one was

---

[34] Keefer, N. (2017). The presence of deficit thinking among social studies educators. *Journal of Social Studies Education Research, 8*(3), 50-75. https://eric.ed.gov/?id=EJ1162277

a White male who taught an urban Title 1 school. These educators were selected for the study because they worked in a large metropolitan area with a 27% Hispanic population and a 17.7% African American population.

After interviewing the teachers over three months and coding their responses to the interview questions, Keefer (2017) concluded that deficit thinking was the primary theme that emerged from the study. Keefer believed the educators' lived experiences (mostly working-class and middle-class) contributed to how they perceived their students (mostly from lower socioeconomic backgrounds). He explained that each educator in the study "utilized deficit language when speaking about people living in poverty" (p. 65).

Keefer's (2017) study indicates a need to effectively prepare educators who will uphold high expectations for culturally diverse students from low socioeconomic backgrounds and combat the impact of deficit thinking on their pedagogy. According to Keefer, an educator's unaddressed deficit thinking might hinder the academic performance of culturally diverse students.[35] Therefore, educators must not only apply a culturally responsive lens to students' racial and ethnic backgrounds but also to

---

[35] Keefer, N. (2017). The presence of deficit thinking among social studies educators. *Journal of Social Studies Education Research, 8*(3), 50-75. https://eric.ed.gov/?id=EJ1162277

students' socioeconomic backgrounds. The goal is to respond appropriately to the needs of each student.

As I have discussed by highlighting Chu's (2016) and Keefer's (2017) work, research illustrates a need to combat negative attitudes and beliefs about culturally diverse students to effectively increase their academic achievement in general and special education settings. Needless to say, this is just one more reason why every educator must seek to become a CRE. CREs are the type of educators who believe in the potential of each learner, and they wholeheartedly reject deficit thinking. Not to mention, CREs understand that every human being has biases, and teachers are no different. Therefore, what separates CREs from others is the fact that they seek to identify their implicit biases to mitigate their impact on students.

So, at this moment, you might be thinking, "I have a better understanding of what constitutes a culturally responsive educator, but why should I seek to become one?" Maybe you are not fully persuaded because you feel that you have been able to help students achieve at a high academic level without employing what you consider "culturally responsive practices." Let's further examine what researchers have to say about the impact of culturally responsive practices on student achievement.

Can Culturally Responsive Teaching Impact Student Achievement?

The positive student outcomes associated with CREs have been well-documented in the research literature over the last 20 years. According to Abacioglu et al. (2020), culturally responsive teaching practices (CRT) have been "found to be related to positive student outcomes, such as increased student engagement, better achievement, and more positive peer relationships" (p. 737).[36] Moreover, CRT has been particularly associated with "increased engagement and interest in school and increased educational achievement of minoritized students" (Abacioglu et al., 2020, p. 737). Aronson and Laughter (2016) summarized over 40 studies related to culturally responsive education and student outcomes. They indicated that CRT helped a plethora of diverse students (African Americans, Latinos, Mexicans, Puerto Ricans, Asians, Native Americans, Iraqis, and other English language learners) become more engaged, motivated, interested in the content, and efficacious in school. Aronson and Laughter asserted that CRT increases the likelihood of students becoming life-long

---

[36] Abacioglu, C.S., Volman, M., & Fisher, A.H. (2020). Teachers' multicultural approaches and perspective taking abilities as factors in culturally responsive teaching. *British Journal of Educational Psychology, 90*(3), 736-752. https://doi.org/10.1111/bjep.12328

learners.[37] Therefore, CRT is not explicitly for African American students; it is the best approach for every child of color.

Many other researchers (Morrell & Duncan-Andrade, 2002; Morrison, 2002; Savage et al., 2011) have also documented the positive impact CRT has on engagement and student success.[38] The positive impact of CRT on student achievement was also noted across content areas. According to Feger (2006) and Souryasack and Lee (2007), teachers reported increases in student engagement in reading and writing when they integrated more culturally relevant literature into the curriculum.[39] Also, several researchers (Dimick, 2012; Johnson, 2011;

---

[37] Aronson, B., & Laughter, J. (2016). The theory and practice of culturally relevant education: A synthesis of research across content areas. *Review of Educational Research, 86*(1), 163-206. https://doi.org/10.3102%2F0034654315582066

[38] Morrell, E., & Jeffrey M. R. Duncan-Andrade. (2002). Promoting academic literacy with urban youth through engaging hip-hop culture. *The English Journal, 91*(6), 88–92. https://doi.org/10.2307/821822
Morrison, J. D. (2002). Using student-generated film to create a culturally relevant community. *The English Journal, 92*(1), 47–52. https://doi.org/10.2307/821946
Savage, C., Hindle, R., Meyer, L.H., Hynds, A., Penetito, W., & Sleeter, C. (2011). Culturally responsive pedagogies in the classroom: indigenous student experiences across the curriculum. *Asia-Pacific Journal of Teacher Education, 39*, 183 - 198. http://dx.doi.org/10.1080/1359866X.2011.588311

[39] Feger, M.V. (2006). "I want to read": How culturally relevant texts increase student engagement in reading. *Multicultural Education, 13*(3), 18-19. https://eric.ed.gov/?id=EJ759630
Souryasack, R., & Lee, J. S. (2007). Drawing on students' experiences, cultures and languages to develop English language writing: Perspectives from three Lao heritage middle school students. *Heritage Language Journal, 5*(1), 79-97. https://eric.ed.gov/?id=EJ831195

Milner, 2011) have indicated that educators were able to successfully engage students in science content knowledge when they employed CRT.[40] Additionally, the positive impact of CRT has also been found in mathematics. Gutstein (2003), Dover (2013), and Hubert (2013) documented increases in student engagement in mathematics when educators employed culturally relevant math instruction.[41] Howard (2020) highlighted how math teachers have used "community issues as a framework for improving math proficiency" (p.70).[42] These findings are noteworthy because many K-12 educators attribute student underperformance to a lack of engagement during explicit and direct instruction. This is likely to be true

---

[40] Dimick, A. S. (2012). Students' empowerment in an environmental science classroom: Toward a framework for social justice science education. *Science Education, 96*, 990–1012. https://doi.org/10.1002/sce.21035
Johnson, C. C. (2011). The road to culturally relevant science: Exploring how teachers navigate change in pedagogy. *Journal of Research in Science Teaching, 48*, 170–198. https://doi.org/10.1002/tea.20405
Milner, H. R. (2011). Culturally relevant pedagogy in a diverse urban classroom. *Urban Review, 43*, 66–89. https://doi.org/10.1007/s11256-009-0143-0
Dover, A. G. (2013). Teaching for social justice: From conceptual frameworks to classroom practices. *Multicultural perspectives, 15*(1), 3-11. https://doi.org/10.1080/15210960.2013.754285
[41] Gutstein, E. (2006). *Reading and writing the world with mathematics: Toward a pedagogy for social justice.* Routledge.
Hubert, T. L. (2013). Learners of mathematics: High school students' perspectives of culturally relevant mathematics pedagogy. *Journal of African American Studies, 18*, 324–336. https://doi.org/10.1007/s12111-013-9273-2
[42] Howard, T. (2020). *Why race and culture matter in schools: Closing the achievement gap in America's classrooms* (2nd ed.). Teachers College Press.

because culturally responsive practices are often absent from the learning environment.

Culturally Responsive Classroom Management

If educators are not persuaded to employ CRT based on the impact it has on student achievement, maybe they will be willing to try it out if they see how it can be an effective approach for minimizing behavioral concerns in the classroom setting. According to Weinstein et al. (2004), culturally responsive classroom management (CRCM) includes five essential components: 1) recognition of one's own ethnocentrism; 2) knowledge of students' cultural backgrounds; 3) understanding of the broader social, economic, and political context; 4) ability and willingness to use culturally appropriate management strategies; and 5) commitment to building caring classrooms (p. 25).[43]

This need for CRCM emerged out of the unequal use of exclusionary discipline practices among culturally diverse students. It has been well-documented since the early 1970s that students of color are suspended more than their White counterparts.[44] While culturally diverse students are often disciplined more frequently and more

---

[43] Weinstein, C. S., Tomlinson-Clarke, S., & Curran, M. (2004). Toward a conception of culturally responsive classroom management. *Journal of Teacher Education, 55* (1), 25–38. https://doi.org/10.1177/0022487103259812

[44] U.S. Department of Education. (2014). *Civil rights data collection, data snapshot: School discipline.* U.S. Department of Education- Office for Civil Rights.

harshly when compared to White students, African American students are disciplined more than any other group. In fact, Smith and Harper (2015) have noted that "In 132 Southern school districts, Blacks were disproportionately suspended at rates five times or higher than their representation in the student population" (p. 1).[45] These discipline inequities concerning Black students are consistent across sex. Black boys are the most suspended subgroup of boys, and Black girls are the most suspended subgroup of girls.[46] These inequities allude to a definite need to assist educators on their journey to become CRE who employ CRCM practices.

Cultural Considerations When Implementing CRCM

Educators must become aware of the differing communication styles among culturally diverse students. African American students are often more accustomed to an active, participatory pattern ("call-response") approach to adult interaction.[47] Meaning African American students often believe it is appropriate to respond to adults without

---

[45] Smith, E. J., & Harper, S. R. (2015). Disproportionate impact of K-12 school suspension and expulsion on Black students in southern states. Philadelphia: *University of Pennsylvania, Center for the Study of Race and Equity in Education.*
[46] Ibid.
[47] Weinstein, C. S., Tomlinson-Clarke, S., & Curran, M. (2004). Toward a conception of culturally responsive classroom management. *Journal of Teacher Education, 55* (1), 25–38. https://doi.org/10.1177/0022487103259812

prompts. In comparison, "European American teachers, for example, are generally accustomed to a 'passive-receptive' discourse pattern; they expect students to listen quietly while the teacher is speaking and then respond individually to a teacher-initiated question" (Weinstein, 2004, p.26). When educators are unaware of these subtle cultural differences, misinterpretations of cultural expressions are likely to lead to problems for students. In many cases, cultural misunderstandings pertaining to African American students often cause them to be deemed disruptive, defiant, non-compliant, and worthy of suspension.

    Weinstein et al. (2004) noted, "Similarly, teachers who do not realize how strongly Pacific Islanders value interpersonal harmony may conclude that these students are lazy when they are reluctant to participate in competitive activities" (p. 26). Without knowledge of cultural differences, educators' perceptions of student behavior can be slanted at best or completely wrong at worst. This is how minor behavioral issues escalate in the classroom setting. Research has indicated that Southeast Asian students may "smile while being scolded" or reprimanded by adults (Weinstein et al., 2004, p.26). Yet, this smile is not meant to be disrespectful but rather an admission of guilt. Weinstein et al. (2004) further explained

> For example, because Latino culture emphasizes the importance of contributing to the group, singling out

individual achievement may be embarrassing and punishing rather than reinforcing. Chastising Filipino American students for a lack of independence can be futile if they have been brought up to depend on adult authority. In addition, reprimanding Chinese American students for not being willing to express their opinions may conflict with their parents' directive to listen and learn what the teacher tells them (p.32).

All of the aforementioned examples confirm the need for educators to foster cultural competence and a basic understanding of students' cultural backgrounds. This understanding will be required if culturally responsive classroom management practices are to effectively be implemented in the classroom. While educators must understand when to accommodate students' cultural backgrounds, they must also understand when to expect students to make accommodations. Nieto (2000) referred to this concept as "mutual accommodation."[48] Mutual accommodation occurs when teachers accept and build on students' cultures but also equip students to function successfully within the culture of the classroom (Nieto, 2000). This, too, is necessary.

---

[48] Nieto, S. (2000). *Affirming diversity: The sociopolitical context of multicultural education* (3rd ed.). Longman.

10 Core Beliefs of CREs

In addition, to the attitudes, beliefs, and expectations of CREs highlighted in this section, Irvine and Armento (2001) explained that CREs adhere to the following 10 core beliefs:

1. "Hold high academic and personal expectations for each child.
2. Provide for each child equitable access to the necessary learning resources and sufficient opportunities to learn.
3. Ensure that learning outcomes are meaningful, relevant, useful, and important to each child.
4. Nurture learning-support communities for each child (families, peers, homework hotlines, community centers).
5. Facilitate the maximum growth of each learner by making informed academic adaptations that match and build upon the learner's prior knowledge, experiences, skills, and beliefs.
6. Build positive and supportive school and classroom learning environments that are grounded in mutual and genuine respect for cultural diversity.
7. Promote classroom climates built on social justice, democracy, and equity.

8. Promote individual empowerment, self-efficacy, positive self-regard, and a belief in societal reform.
9. Value diversity as well as human commonalities.
10. Believe that it is their role and responsibility to provide effective and empowering instruction for each child." (p. 23)[49]

---

[49] Irvine J. J., & Armento, B. J. (2001). *Culturally responsive teaching*. McGraw-Hill.

Summary of Section 1: Culturally Responsive Educators

As mentioned previously, public school teachers in today's schools are expected to provide a quality education for the most diverse group of K-12 students in our nation's history. This is most definitely a challenging task. Yet, it is not impossible. CREs must be developed and trained. Every child deserves to be supported by individuals who view their cultural background as an asset and not a liability. Every child deserves to be instructed by an educator who has the ability to integrate students' cultural knowledge, prior experiences, frames of reference, and performance styles within the classroom to make learning encounters more relevant to and effective for them.[50] CREs are educators who commit to building meaningful relationships with students. They intentionally seek to diversify their knowledge base with the goal of becoming culturally competent. Additionally, they embrace beliefs and expectations that allow them to successfully engage in culturally responsive and culturally affirming actions. These actions include teaching with a high level of rigor and employing CRCM practices. To be clear, developing CREs will not be an easy or quick task. It will take time and an intentional, strategic, and sequential

---

[50] Gay, G. (2018). *Culturally responsive teaching: Theory, research, and practice* (3rd ed.). Teachers College Press.

professional development plan. In the next section, I will articulate the five steps that I believe must be taken if CREs are to be developed.

Extension Questions for Educators to Consider:
1. What is your favorite strategy for building relationships and establishing a positive rapport with the students you serve?
2. Based on what you have learned in this section, how would you describe a culturally responsive educator (CRE)?
3. Do you think diverse students require CREs to achieve at a high academic level? Why?
4. What might be a barrier to an educator's ability to become a CRE?
5. What is the relationship between academic achievement gaps and gaps in culturally responsive instruction? In other words, is it really an academic achievement gap, or is it a gap in culturally responsive instruction?
6. How might discipline issues in schools be used as a metric to help educators evaluate the school's ability to be culturally responsive?
7. Do you think integrating culturally responsive instruction with specially designed instruction will

have a positive impact on culturally diverse students with disabilities?

Section 2: Five Necessary Action Steps

Essential Question: What are the five necessary action steps that every educator must take if they are seeking to become a Culturally Responsive Educator (CRE)?

5 Necessary Action Steps to Become a Culturally Responsive Educator (CRE)

STEP 1
Develop Historical Awareness

STEP 2
Foster Multicultural Consciousness

STEP 3
Apply Culturally Responsive Approaches

STEP 4
Prioritize Family and Community Engagement

STEP 5
Advocate for Culturally Responsive Schools

Purpose Pushers LLC 2023 | www.purposepushers.com | Dr. Jahkari Taylor

Step 1: Develop Historical Awareness

Step 1 - Develop Historical Awareness

"More than 600 Black schools were burned in the South between 1864-1876."
- JARVIS R. GIVENS

"A people without the knowledge of their past history, origin, and culture is like a tree without roots."
- MARCUS GARVEY

Essential Question: What role does history play in becoming culturally responsive?

My personal journey to become a CRE was inspired by the discovery of what I deemed to be "profound historical facts" about education. This was not an instantaneous event but rather a cumulative process that occurred over time. As a teenager, I learned that one of the first universities in world history was founded in the African city of Timbuktu.[51] For some reason, this revelation created a type of "cognitive dissonance" within me. Cognitive dissonance refers to disordered emotions that

---

[51] Hammer, J. (2006). The treasures of Timbuktu. *Smithsonian, 37*(9), 46–57. https://www.smithsonianmag.com/history/the-treasures-of-timbuktu-138566090/

result from cognitive inconsistencies.[52] I was amazed, proud, and perplexed all at the same time, but my disordered state of mind was due to the fact that I had never been exposed to any references to African brilliance, genius, or scholarship in school. The omission of this profound historical fact made me wonder what else had been omitted from my schooling experience.

  Once I arrived on a college campus, I was exposed to more profound historical facts. As soon as I enrolled at Norfolk State University, a Historically Black College/University (HBCU), I was required to take an entry-level history class, which exposed me to the knowledge of "anti-literacy laws." I learned that the United States government attempted to systematically reproduce ignorance by prohibiting Black people from learning in the antebellum South. Literally, it was a crime to teach Black people to read and write in seven states in the South.[53] Again, this was a profound revelation for me because I had never heard of any of this information during my K-12 experience. These are just a few profound historical facts about education that set the stage for me to become a CRE. In this Step, I hope to provide you with a few

---

[52] Zhang, S., & Pan, Y. (2023). Mind over matter: Examining the role of cognitive dissonance and self-efficacy in discontinuous usage intentions on pan-entertainment mobile live broadcast platforms. *Behavioral Sciences (2076-328X), 13*(3), 254. https://doi.org/10.3390/bs13030254
[53] Tolley, K. (2016). Slavery. In A. J. Angulo (Ed.), *Miseducation: A history of ignorance-making in American and abroad* (pp. 13-33). Johns Hopkins University Press.

profound historical facts about education that will help you understand why becoming a CRE begins with the development of historical awareness.

Educators Need Historical Awareness

The first step toward becoming a CRE begins with historical awareness. Historical awareness, in this context, refers to "an awareness of the historical and sociopolitical events that inspired the current push for culturally responsive teaching in schools." In other words, one must ask, "How did we get here? What historical events served as catalysts for the emergence of culturally responsive teaching?" As we investigate and research historical and sociopolitical events in American history, particularly those events that have impacted the educational system, we will begin to see why becoming culturally responsive is a popular topic in modern educational discussions.

Understanding the Foundation of Educational Inequity

The first public school in America dedicated to educating American youth was a high school named the Boston Latin School.[54] It was established in 1635 in Boston, Massachusetts. This school focused on teaching

---

[54] Mulligan, H. A. (1985, Apr 07). *Boston's Latin school thriving in 350th year: [Bulldog Edition].* Los Angeles Times.

students basic academic skills and core religious values, but it was not an inclusive institution. Black, indigenous, and other students of color were excluded from attending. In fact, the first Black graduates of the Boston Latin School were Parker Bailey in 1877 and Clement Morgan in 1886.[55] This means the first public school in American history took 242 years to provide just one Black student an opportunity to graduate. Since the original intention of American schools was to exclude Black, indigenous, and other students of color from receiving an education, one can conclude that the foundation was not originally structured and built for equality or equity. Historically, American schools have always resisted providing equitable opportunities to students of color.

Consider the fact that while White students were seated in classrooms being exposed to rich and rigorous learning opportunities designed to hone their cognitive abilities, Black students were cognitively stifled by abject poverty and the traumatic experiences related to chattel slavery. While White students were greeted by friendly faces as they walked the halls in the school corridors, Black students were met with anger, rage, and physical violence while walking the cotton fields on a plantation. These images paint a stark contrast between the learning

---

[55] The Boston Banner. (2016). *The real problem at BLS: too few black applicants.* https://www.baystatebanner.com/2016/10/12/the-real-problem-at-bls-too-few-black-applicants/

experiences of White and Black youth from the early 1600s to the late 1800s. Yet, things would eventually start to change for Black students.

Three Important Lessons from the First Black Public High School

After the Civil War ended in 1865, Congress ratified the 13th Amendment, which states, "Neither slavery nor involuntary servitude, except as a punishment for crime whereof the party shall have been duly convicted, shall exist within the United States, or any place subject to their jurisdiction."[56] The abolition of slavery was a significant event that had tremendous implications for how Black youth would be educated in America. This precedent-setting law provided motivation for citizens to begin erecting public learning institutions to help Black students learn, grow, and hone their cognitive capacities. Five years after the ramification of the 13th Amendment, the first Black public high school opened its doors in 1870 in Washington, D.C.[57] This school, currently named Paul Laurence Dunbar High School after one of America's most gifted poets, was

---

[56] U.S. Constitution. Amendment. XIII.
[57] Moore, C. A. (2014, Jul). *First class: The legacy of dunbar, America's first black public high school.* Lawrence Hill Books.

originally named the Preparatory High School for Colored Youth and later named M Street School.[58]

From 1891-1916, the M Street School provided dynamic learning opportunities for Black students, which caused these students to achieve tremendous academic success. In 1899, a test was given to four public high schools in Washington, three White schools, and the M Street School. According to Sowell (1899), the M Street school scored higher than two of the three White high schools. Needless to say, the M Street School was helping Black students demonstrate the highest levels of academic achievement. According to Davis (2010), the M Street School "was one of the most prestigious and exceptional African American educational institutions to have ever existed in the United States" (p. 2).[59] You might be asking, "How did the educators at the M Street School inspire African American students to achieve such a high level of academic success while being confronted by Jim Crow, segregation, and discrimination?"

The M Street School was led by dynamic educational leaders who held fast to high expectations for the students they sought to serve. In addition, these

---

[58] Robinson, H. S. (1983). The M street high school, 1891-1916. *Records of the Columbia Historical Society, 51,* 119-143. https://doi.org/10.2307/40067848

[59] Davis, R. (2010). The M street school, 1896-1916. *The Ohio State University, Beverly M. Gordon College of Education and Human Ecology.* https://u.osu.edu/gordon.3/files/2012/06/PRalph-Davis.pdf

leaders were determined to hire the best, most qualified teachers, many of which had earned Ph.Ds. Two of the most famous teachers at the M Street School were Parker Bailey and Carter G. Woodson. Bailey, the aforementioned first Black graduate of the Boston Latin School, was also a graduate of Harvard College. Carter G. Woodson, who is the second African American to have earned his Ph.D. from Harvard, is also known as the "father of Black history." Describing the effectiveness of the nation's first Black public high school, Stewart (2015) stated,

> teachers developed generations of highly educated, high-achieving African Americans, groundbreakers that included the first Black member of a presidential cabinet, the first Black graduate of the US Naval Academy, the first Black army general, the creator of the modern blood bank, the first Black state attorney general, the legal mastermind behind school desegregation, and hundreds of educators.[60]

When I analyze the effectiveness of the M Street School as a learning institution that was able to increase the academic achievement of Black students during a racially challenging and socio-politically charged time, I notice three essential components woven into its fabric. *Number 1:* The M Street School was led by excellent educational leadership who possessed historical

---

[60] Stewart, A. (2015). *First class: The legacy of dunbar, America's first black public high school.* Lawrence Hill Books.

awareness, demonstrated empathy, and communicated high expectations.[61] *Number 2:* The M Street School was able to recruit, hire, develop, and retain the most qualified educators. *Number 3:* The M Street School embodied a collective determination to succeed. Every member of that educational community was willing to do whatever it would take to help the students demonstrate progress at the highest level. They believed in the students, and they were determined to see their students demonstrate success. They were so ambitious that they started in 1870 with four students in the basement of a church! They did not wait for a beautiful, modern school with classrooms possessing flexible seating arrangements and the best technological gadgets.

It is also important to remember that the M Street School accomplished great success during the late 1800s and early 1900s before the *Brown vs. Board of Education* court case, which means they were operating in excellence in a segregated context. The point of the matter is modern narratives of academic achievement gaps were nonexistent at the M Street School, and I believe they can be nonexistent in the schools of today if we are willing to learn from the nation's first Black public high school.

---

[61] NPR Staff. (2013 July 29). *In nation's First black public school, A blueprint for reform.* NPR
https://www.npr.org/sections/codeswitch/2013/08/22/206622688/the-legacy-of-dunbar-high-school

Brown Vs. Board of Education

During a time when schools were still segregated by race, the M Street School graduated around 80% of its African American student body.[62] This was certainly unprecedented, and I am sure most people who were acquainted with the success of the M Street School believed in their hearts that ending segregation would lead to even greater success for African American students. The argument leading up to the *Brown v. Board of Education* (1954) case was rooted in the fact that separating students by race leads to unequal protection under the law, unequal access to facilities, and unequal access to resources.[63] In other words, inequity in the educational system was being maintained by laws that permitted segregation in schools which had an adverse impact on African American students. Therefore, educators, legal scholars, and community activists of that day took their fight to the Supreme Court. They fought long and hard to end legalized segregation in schools. Chief Justice Warren delivered his opinion to the court by stating,

> Segregation of white and colored children in public schools has a detrimental effect upon the colored

---

[62] Ysrayl, Y. (2018 July 27). Black history fun fact Friday - the first black public high school. *Medium.* https://medium.com/@yecheilyah/black-history-fun-fact-friday-the-first-black-public-high-school-d8628cace434
[63] Brown v. Board of Education, 347 U.S. 483 (1954). https://www.oyez.org/cases/1940-1955/347us483

children. The impact is greater when it has the sanction of the law, for the policy of separating the races is usually interpreted as denoting the inferiority of the negro group. A sense of inferiority affects the motivation of a child to learn. Segregation with the sanction of law, therefore, has a tendency to [retard] the educational and mental development of negro children and to deprive them of some of the benefits they would receive in a racially integrated school system... We conclude that, in the field of public education, the doctrine of "separate but equal" has no place. Separate educational facilities are inherently unequal (p. 496).[64]

Unintended Consequences of Integration

No doubt about it, the precedent-setting Supreme Court ruling in the *Brown v. Board of Education* case was a positive step in the right direction concerning equality in schools. Early research indicated positive effects related to desegregation, such as an increase in short-term academic achievement for White and Black students as well as positive cross-racial interactions.[65] However, it is important to mention that over 38,000 African American

---

[64] Brown v. Board of Education, 347 U.S. 483 (1954).
[65] Braddock II, J. H., & Eitle, T. M. (2004). The effects of school desegregation. In Banks, J. A., & Banks, C. A. M. (2004). *Handbook of research on multicultural education. 2nd ed.* (pp. 828-840). Jossey-Bass.

educators lost their jobs when schools were integrated.[66] While the courts pushed the nation toward integration, most White educational leaders were reluctant to hire African American teachers. Not to mention, the vast majority of Black principals who formerly served as leaders of all-Black schools were not viewed as qualified enough to lead newly integrated schools. Therefore, it is safe to say school integration was literally the inception of the teacher shortage concerning African American educators.

Massive Resistance

Not only did *Brown v. Board of Education* unintentionally contribute to the teacher shortage, but it also inspired some political leaders to place the educational system into the crosshairs of heated political discourse. During the 1950s, politicians started using laws, policies, and political power to keep schools segregated. This became known as *Massive Resistance*.[67] Massive Resistance was literally a group of laws passed in 1956 to defy *Brown v. Board of Education* and maintain racial segregation in schools. According to Coleman (2018), Massive Resistance "aimed to abolish the public school

---

[66] Lutz, M. (2017). The hidden cost of Brown v. Board: African American educators' resistance to desegregating schools. *Online Journal of Rural Research & Policy, 12*(4). https://doi.org/10.4148/1936-0487.1085

[67] Epps-Robertson, C. (2016). The race to erase Brown v. Board of Education: The Virginia way and the rhetoric of massive resistance. *Rhetoric Review, 35*(2), 108–120. http://dx.doi.org/10.1080/07350198.2016.1142812

system and replace it with a private school system for Whites only" (p. 1).[68] Massive Resistance is of personal interest to me because it originated in my home state of Virginia. Harry F. Byrd, Sr., the U.S. senator representing Virginia, was its most vocal proponent. Senator Byrd promoted the "Southern Manifesto," which was signed in 1956 by over 100 Southern congressmen who also opposed integration.[69]

Under Massive Resistance, a "Pupil Placement Board was created with the power to assign specific students to particular schools" (page 1).[70] In addition, tuition grants were provided to families who opposed integration. The grants would allow students to attend the segregated school of their choice. While these events are all noteworthy and thought-provoking, the most extreme component of Massive Resistance was a law that cut off state funds and closed any public school that attempted to integrate.[71] School closures across the entire state of Virginia ensued. Consequently, thousands of White and

---

[68] Coleman, A. L. (May 16, 2018). *The county that closed its public schools rather than desegregate after Brown v. Board of Education.* Time. https://time.com/5277732/brown-board-education-prince-edward-county/
[69] Epps-Robertson, C. (2016). The race to erase Brown v. Board of Education: The Virginia way and the rhetoric of massive resistance. *Rhetoric Review, 35*(2), 108–120. http://dx.doi.org/10.1080/07350198.2016.1142812
[70] Virginia Museum of History & Culture. (2023). *Massive resistance.* https://virginiahistory.org/learn/historical-book/chapter/massive-resistance
[71] Ibid.

Black students were locked out of schools without an opportunity to receive an education.

These school closures dealt a devastating blow to the academic achievement of so many students. Some districts in Virginia closed schools for years. In Prince Edward County, Virginia, school officials closed public schools for five years.[72] Let's relate this occurrence in a modern context: Many educators who endured teaching during the Covid-19 pandemic have lamented about the "loss of learning" that was a consequence of just one year of fully virtual instruction. If we compare that one year of virtual instruction to five years with no instruction at all, we can only imagine how student achievement was stifled by school closures associated with massive resistance. Consider how closing schools over a five-year period may have impacted student achievement, particularly the most marginalized populations. According to Coleman (2018), this period of massive resistance was an intensely challenging time for parents and students. Coleman (2018) asserted, "Some students discontinued their education [altogether]." While all students in Virginia were impacted by school closures, we must understand that the impact on African American communities was most severe. White

---

[72] Coleman, A. L. (2018) The county that closed its public schools rather than desegregate after *Brown v. Board of Education*.
https://www.yahoo.com/news/county-closed-public-schools-rather-150003990.html

students were able to receive tuition grants and attend private schools, while African American students were left to fend for themselves without a school to attend. Massive Resistance undoubtedly contributed to the achievement gaps that CREs seek to close today. (*For a more comprehensive understanding of the chronology related to school segregation in Virginia, please search online for the* Desegregation of Virginia Education (DOVE): Timeline - Old Dominion University (odu.edu)).

    Discussing Virginia's role in Massive Resistance, Clark (2021) stated, "Virginia's most famous public education moment – its participation in 'Massive Resistance' in the years following *Brown V. Board of Education*—instead showed the Commonwealth's willingness to sacrifice its children's education to hold onto the racist ideals of its past" (p. 1118).[73] Unfortunately, similar circumstances which accelerated inequities in schools were replicated across the United States, impacting Native American, Hispanic, and other minoritized populations. Therefore, it is imperative for CREs to develop historical awareness pertaining to the context in which they are situated. By developing historical awareness, educators will be better equipped to take a more

---

[73] Clark, J. B. (2021). From massive resistance to quiet evasion: The struggle for educational equity and integration in Virginia. *Virginia Law Review, 107*(5), 1115–1164. https://virginialawreview.org/articles/from-massive-resistance-to-quiet-evasion-the-struggle-for-educational-equity-and-integration-in-virginia/

empathetic and compassionate approach to meet the needs of students, families, and communities that have been marginalized throughout history.

Shifting the Focus of Scholars

In response to the sociopolitical consequences surrounding the *Brown v. Board of Education* decision, African American scholarship shifted toward changing the educational system as a whole. During that time in American history, 85% of our nation's population was White, 11% was Black, less than 4% was Latino, and less than 6% was foreign-born.[74] In other words, America's racial-ethnic makeup was not as diverse as it is today, which is why most of the emphasis within educational reform was on African American students. Therefore, after the *Brown v. Board of Education* case was passed, scholars no longer had to brainstorm and strategize new ways to integrate African American students into a desegregated school system. Instead, they started

---

[74] Sabet, R. F. (2023). *CCF civil rights symposium: Changes in America's racial and ethnic composition since 1964.* https://sites.utexas.edu/contemporaryfamilies/2014/02/05/changes-in-americas-racial-and-ethnic-composition-since-1964/#:~:text=In%20the%20early%201960s%2C%2085,in%20America's%20racial%2Dethnic%20makeup

focusing on how and what students would be taught in these newly desegregated educational spaces.[75]

African American scholars and practitioners quickly realized that Congress successfully legislated school integration, but it could not legislate hearts and minds. Thus, many educational leaders in Black communities voiced concerns about White teachers upholding negative attitudes and beliefs about African American students. According to Marshall (2019), some African American community leaders of the 1960s "worried that White teachers would be unable to let go of their thoughts about the inferiority of Black children" (p. 72).[76] This notion led many to believe that negative attitudes, beliefs, and dispositions about African American students would become barriers to their achievement.

The Emergence of Multicultural Education

The multicultural education movement of today was inspired by the historical context of the past. According to Banks and Banks (2004), multicultural education is "a field of study and an emerging discipline whose major aim is to

---

[75] Gay, G. (2004). Beyond brown: Promoting equality through multicultural education. *Journal of Curriculum and Supervision, 19*(3), 193-216. https://eric.ed.gov/?id=EJ732626

[76] Marshall, T. R. (2019). Desegregated schools, unequal assignments. *Educational Leadership, 76* (7), 72. https://www.ascd.org/el/articles/desegregated-schools-unequal-assignments

create equal educational opportunities for students from diverse racial, ethnic, social-class, and cultural groups" (p. xi).[77] One of the goals of multicultural education is to "actualize for all the ideals that the founding fathers intended for an elite few at the nation's birth (p. xi)."[78] The contemporary manifestation of the multicultural education movement emerged during the 1960s as a response to school integration. It was born out of frustration and concern that African American students and other minoritized students would be treated unfairly in the newly integrated schools. Keep in mind many of the same teachers who protested integration would now be responsible for educating African American students. Many educational leaders who had been led to believe for years that African Americans were aloof, racially inferior to Whites, and mentally incapable of learning alongside White students would now be expected to provide a quality education for Black students. This thought concerned many members of the African American community. Therefore, researchers became increasingly interested in investigating what takes place inside schools concerning the education of diverse students. This focus on what (curriculum) and how (pedagogy) culturally diverse youth

---

[77] Banks, J. A., & Banks, C. A. M. (2004). *Handbook of research on multicultural education*. 2nd ed. Jossey-Bass.
[78] Ibid.

are being taught in school remains an important topic of interest to researchers today.[79]

The Need for Culturally Responsive Curricula

It should not be a shocking revelation to understand how the values of the multicultural education movement, which focused on appreciating diversity and providing equal access to all, would eventually progress toward challenging the curriculum in schools. According to Capella-Santana (2003), "The curriculum in the United States has been based historically on the European American perspective" (p. 183).[80] In terms of diversity in the curriculum, minority perspectives are often represented in a limited fashion across core content areas and non-core classes (Link, 2019).[81] In fact, from the inception of public schools in America to the passage of *Brown v. Board of Education*, people of color have historically been omitted from the school curriculum. Yet, the multicultural education movement, fueled by the Civil Rights Movement

---

[79] Delpit, L. (2006). *Other people's children: Cultural conflict in the classroom*. The New Press.
Gay, G. (2018). *Culturally responsive teaching*. Teachers College Press.
[80] Capella-Santana, N. (2003). Voices of teacher candidates: Positive changes in multicultural attitudes and knowledge. *The Journal of Educational Research, 96*(3), 182-189. https://doi.org/10.1080/00220670309598806
[81] Link, B. (2019). White lies: Unraveling whiteness in the elementary art curriculum. *Journal of Research in Art Education, 36*(3), 11-28. https://doi.org/10.2458/jcrae.4808

of the 1960s and its push for inclusion across American society, set the stage for advocates to start demanding representation in the curriculum. Similar to my student who asked, "Are there any Hispanic scientists," many Americans during the 1960s became increasingly aware of groups who were missing from the school curriculum.

Fitzgerald and Lauter (2004) stated, "Civil rights activists and students asked of courses of study, especially at mostly White institutions, 'Where are the Blacks?' And later, 'Where are the women?' 'Where are we in your texts, your bookshelves, your syllabi, your classrooms, and faculties?'" (p. 910).[82] At the time, the curriculum rarely depicted diverse individuals in a positive manner. Researchers such as Pilgrim (2000) and Gay (2004) asserted that the curriculum in public schools during the 19th century often perpetuated racist stereotypes.[83] According to Gay (2004), the school curriculum often portrayed African Americans as "docile, ignorant simpletons and childlike creatures; Native Americans were seen as uncivilized or noble savages to be civilized by Europeans; and Mexican Americans were presented as lazy and untrustworthy people who spoke virtually unintelligible English" (p. 200). The fragmented

---

[82] Fitzgerald, A. K., & Lauter, P. (2004). Multiculturalism and the core curricula. In J. A. Banks & C. A. M. Banks (2004). *Handbook of research on multicultural education. 2nd ed.* (pp. 906-930). Jossey-Bass.
[83] Pilgrim, D. (2000). *The brute caricature.* Ferris State University. https://www.ferris.edu/jimcrow/brute/

representation and negative portrayals of minority cultures in textbooks not only perpetuated stereotypes but also prevented students from seeing the brilliance and genius within every culture.

This recognition led researchers to work toward developing culturally relevant curricula (Gay, 2002).[84] Culturally relevant curricula refer to instructional tools and resources such as textbooks that are culturally affirming for diverse students. The goal of culturally relevant and responsive curricula is to empower students, as opposed to disempowering and making students feel less significant or inferior (Ladson-Billings, 2009; Taylor, 2022).[85] If students are expected to possess skills associated with critical thinking, creative thinking, collaboration, communication, and citizenship, educators must be willing to teach with that purpose in mind. Yet, educators will never be rooted in that purpose if they fail to take into account how we arrived at this particular juncture in public education.

---

[84] Gay, G. (2002). Preparing for culturally responsive teaching. *Journal of Teacher Education, 53*(2), 106-116. https://doi.org/10.1177%2F0022487102053002003
[85] Taylor, J. H. (2022). *Relationship between multicultural consciousness and culturally responsive teaching self-efficacy* (Publication No. 30241427) [Doctoral dissertation, Regent University]. ProQuest Dissertations & Theses Global.

The Past Puts the Present in Context

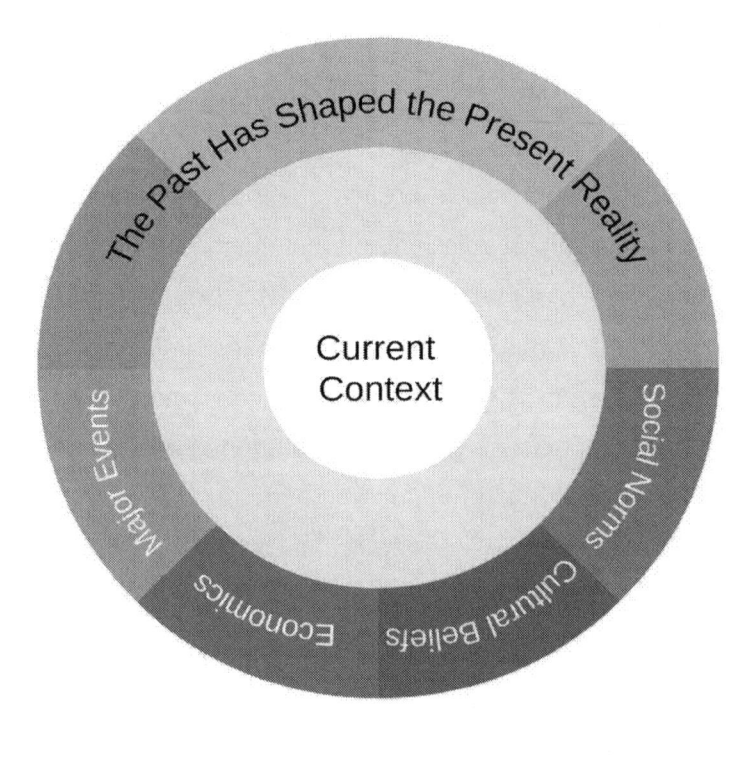

The Past Has Shaped the Present Reality

- Social Norms
- Cultural Beliefs
- Economics
- Major Events

Current Context

Purpose Pushers LLC 2023 | www.purposepushers.com | Dr. Jahkari Taylor

Summary of Step 1: Develop Historical Awareness

The aim of this section, Develop Historical Awareness, was to provide context so educators may understand how we arrived at this particular place and time in history as it relates to the education of culturally diverse youth. In a nutshell, foundational inequities led to the establishment of the first segregated public school for Black students. The success of the first public school for Black students provided promise and stoked an imagination of greater possibilities which caused communities of color to rally in support of the *Brown v. Board of Education* case. Then, the multicultural education movement fueled by the Civil Rights Movement of the 1960s and 1970s eventually gave birth to the current movement in education, calling for *culturally responsive teaching* (CRT) and the need to develop CREs in schools. This work is even more important in today's schools because educators must now be able to respond appropriately to a more culturally diverse student body. According to Sabet (2023), "The biggest change since 1964 has been the growing diversification in America's racial-ethnic makeup" (p. 1).[86] In step two, I argue that

---

[86] Sabet, R. F. (2023). CCF civil rights symposium: Changes in America's racial and ethnic composition since 1964.

educators who desire to become CREs must develop not only historical awareness but also *foster multicultural consciousness*.

Extension Questions for Educators to Consider:

1. What are your thoughts about the time period in our nation's history when students of color were prohibited from attending public schools?
2. How might achievement gaps be related to historical inequities concerning the education of students of color?
3. What are your thoughts about how school closures as a protest to integration might have contributed to the modern concept of "achievement gaps?"
4. How might anti-literacy laws of the 18th century be related to literacy issues plaguing minoritized communities of today?
5. What is the relationship between the small number of African American teachers in schools today and the almost 40,000 African American educators who lost their job as a consequence of school integration?

---

https://sites.utexas.edu/contemporaryfamilies/2014/02/05/changes-in-americas-racial-and-ethnic-composition-since-1964/#:~:text=In%20the%20early%201960s%2C%2085,in%20America's%20racial%2Dethnic%20makeup

6. What are your thoughts about the need for diverse representation in textbooks and other teaching resources?
7. Are you able to identify which cultural groups are excluded from your school's curriculum?

Step 2: Foster Multicultural Consciousness

Step 2 - Foster Multicultural Consciousness

"We do not really see through our eyes or hear through our ears, but through our beliefs."
- *LISA DELPIT*

"In diversity, there is beauty and there is strength."
- *MAYA ANGELOU*

Essential Question: Are my attitudes and beliefs about cultural diversity assets or liabilities for diverse students?

In the first section, my aim was to introduce and explore research related to cultural responsiveness with the goal of developing a concrete definition of what constitutes a culturally responsive educator (CRE). Using existing research, I established concrete actions and practices that must be demonstrated by CREs. In addition, I explained why CREs are necessary for every student in every school. Then in Step One of the Five Necessary Actions Steps for Becoming a CRE, I established that developing historical awareness (an understanding of the sociopolitical and historical context that paved the way for the emergence of cultural responsiveness in education) must be foundational for every CRE. Now in Step Two, we will examine the need for culturally responsive attitudes, beliefs, and dispositions. Since actions are the fruit that grows from the soil of our attitudes and beliefs, it is important to embrace a mindset that is conducive to the effective application of culturally responsive practices. As Lisa Delpit so eloquently articulated, "We do not really see through our eyes or hear through our ears but through our beliefs." Therefore, in this step, I will argue that attitudes, beliefs, and dispositions precede the effective application of culturally responsive practices, meaning they are the prerequisites.

Beneath the Surface

As an educational consultant that has provided professional development services, executive coaching, and keynotes across the nation, I have witnessed many educational leaders engage in "check-the-box" approaches to becoming culturally responsive. I define a check-the-box approach as any stand-alone, one day, or short-term attempt to engage adults in culturally responsive professional development without a long-term and sustained action plan. This is a check-the-box approach because it is not possible to go deeper into the work of becoming culturally responsive without a sequential plan to build capacity. Educational leaders must lead the charge of helping educators engage in what Dr. Yolanda Sealy-Ruiz referred to as "the archeology of self" (p. 22).[87] According to Sealy-Ruiz (2022), the archeology of self refers to "a deep excavation and exploration of beliefs, biases, and ideas that shape how we engage in our work" (p. 22). In other words, educators must be willing to grab their proverbial shovels and dig deep into their hearts and minds to explore what might be implicitly embedded in their values and beliefs. This deep inner work can only be done when individual educators engage in critical self-reflection.

Where do we begin... Unpacking Our Stories

Educators can begin the process of increasing their self-awareness by critically reflecting on their stories. The reality is every person has a story based on the lived experiences that have shaped their values, beliefs, and overall identity. These experiences started during our childhood and have exerted a massive influence on who we are today. So, educators can start unpacking their stories by asking themselves the following questions: "What are the key experiences that have shaped my life? Who are the key people that have contributed to who I am today? What are the key events or institutions that have influenced my values and beliefs?" By exploring questions

---

[87] Sealey-Ruiz, Y. (2022). An archaeology of self for our times: Another talk to teachers. *English Journal, 111*(5), 21-26. https://library.ncte.org/journals/EJ/issues/v111-5

like these, educators can start unpacking their stories. Let me model for you how this critical reflection might look.

My Story

Today, I am an adult, Christian, African American male who also happens to be a husband and father to five beautiful children. I was born in New York City, but my family relocated to Virginia when I was around five years old. Our relocation was prompted by a traumatic life event. My uncle was involved in a horrific car accident as he traveled from New York to Florida. He was not wearing a seatbelt, and therefore he was ejected through the front windshield of the vehicle. He had deep lacerations on his face and broken bones and was in need of a metal rod inserted into his hip. The site of the car accident was in close proximity to the Chesapeake Bay Bridge, which was two hours away from the nearest emergency medical center. Therefore, the Nightingale Regional Air Ambulance was dispatched to airlift my uncle to the Sentara Norfolk General Hospital in Norfolk, Virginia.

My family received a phone call from the medical professionals explaining what transpired and encouraged us to visit my uncle in the hospital because he would require a number of emergency surgeries. The doctors were not assured that he would survive; therefore, they advised us to visit the hospital immediately if possible.

Following the call, my mother packed a few of our belongings, and we drove from New York to Virginia in a 1987 Ford Fairmont that we nicknamed "Betsy." Little did we know, Betsy would soon become our place of residence. We did not have any family or friends living in Virginia at that time. In addition, we were extremely poor. My mother was a single parent trying her best to raise two boys when this traumatic experience occurred.

      After a couple of weeks of living in Betsy, we relocated to a congested homeless shelter in Norfolk. My brother and I would attend our elementary school after sleeping each night in the shelter. Although I was just a kindergartener, I vividly remember that experience. After my first year in school, my mother applied for a federal housing choice voucher, better known as "Section 8." According to the U.S. Department of Housing and Urban Development, "The housing choice voucher program is the federal government's major program for assisting very low-income families, the elderly, and the disabled to afford decent, safe, and sanitary housing in the private market."[88] This voucher afforded us an opportunity to leave the shelter and move into an apartment of our own.

---

[88] U.S. Department of Housing and Urban Development. (2023). *Housing choice vouchers fact sheet.* https://www.hud.gov/topics/housing_choice_voucher_program_section_8

My Upbringing and K-12 Experience

With only a few options available where the housing voucher was accepted as payment, we eventually settled in a socioeconomically deprived community in the South Norfolk borough of Chesapeake, Virginia. The South Norfolk borough of Chesapeake had the highest poverty and crime rates in the city. Nonetheless, we moved into an apartment complex that was named Wilmund Place Apartments. It was in this neighborhood that my mother continued to raise my brother and me. On the very first day of school in my new neighborhood, my brother was jumped on and violently beaten by four boys. When he came home with tears in his eyes, expressing pain, anger, and frustration about what he had experienced, I felt my youthful rage increasing within me. It was in that moment that my innocence left me, and aggression took root. From that point on, I was ready for whatever would confront us in this community.

As I matriculated from elementary to middle school, I became less interested in school and more interested in sports. My mother signed me up for organized football with a local recreation center, and I instantly became infatuated with the physical nature of the sport. At the end of that year, I tried out for the middle school football team and earned a spot. My coaches were the best role models I had during my early years. They taught me the importance of goal-setting, teamwork, determination, resilience, commitment, and other key values that would become staples of my identity. While I would describe my upbringing as fun, secure, and overwhelmingly positive, I did not thrive in school. In fact, I put forth very little effort toward academic excellence.

By the time I became a high school student, I was completely detached from school. I skipped school almost every Friday during my freshman year. When I was present, I was more determined to socialize with friends than I was to complete assignments. I believe I was stuck in "survival mode," constantly trying to prove that I was no pushover. Needless to say, I was underperforming at the highest level. My cumulative grade point average at the end of my ninth-grade year was 0.75. I literally maintained an "F average." I was not eligible to play any sports, which was the key to my personal joy and motivation at that time. Yet, things would change soon.

At the end of my sophomore year, I met the newly hired football coach who persuaded me to try out for the team. This coach showed interest in me in and out of school. He convinced me to take courses during summer school to increase my grade point average so I could become eligible to play varsity football, which I did. In my first year on the team, I earned a starting position playing Wide Receiver and Cornerback. In addition, we finished that year with only one loss. The next year we went undefeated and became district champions for the first time in my school's history.

As my senior year was coming to an end, my coach approached me and said, "JT, where do you want to go to college?" I literally laughed and said, "Coach, I'm not going to college. College isn't for me, plus no one in my community goes to college." He responded, "Son, you are definitely going to college." Although he was adamant about me attending college, I struggled internally to believe that I was "college material." A few college recruiters visited my house and spoke with my family about me attending their university. Out of the coaches who came to visit, I personally connected with a Wide Receiver coach from Christopher Newport University (CNU). This coach made me feel like I had a chance to succeed on and off the field, so I made the decision to enroll at Christopher Newport University in Newport News, Virginia. This is where I would begin my journey as a college student.

My Experiences in College

Upon enrolling at CNU, I became a teenage father. I was literally at practice when my coach received a phone call that my son's mother was going into labor. I vividly remember speeding to the hospital in the passenger side of my coach's Ford Mustang. We arrived at the hospital just in time for me to witness the birth of my firstborn son. I was 17 years old at the time. So, not only did I have the identity of an impoverished young man from the inner city of South Norfolk, but I also was a teenage father who had no clue about fatherhood. This was primarily the case because I was raised without a father in a community with few father figures and positive male role models. Nevertheless, I was determined to ensure that my son would grow up with his father present in his life. So, my strategy was to return home from college each weekend to make sure I spent quality time with my son. While this helped my relationship with my son, it added pressure to my experience as a college student.

You can only imagine how challenging my first semester of college was. By the end of that semester, I found myself on academic probation. It literally felt like I was experiencing my freshman year of high school all over again, but only this time on a college campus. Similar to my freshman year in high school, academic detachment and withdrawal ensued. This situation was exacerbated by the fact that I did not have many friendships at CNU. CNU was nothing like my high school.

Whereas my high school contained a large percentage of African American students, in terms of student racial demographics, most of the students at CNU identified racially as White. Additionally, where students in my high school might have been racially different, most of us shared the same socioeconomic background. We were all predominantly impoverished. Some may have lived in apartments, some lived in trailers, and some lived in small houses on the same street as the apartments, but poverty was a common connection. However, the vast majority of the students I encountered at CNU were not from the Hampton Roads Region of Virginia. Most were from middle-class neighborhoods in Northern Virginia.

During my first two years at CNU, I did not have the vocabulary to describe my internal battle, but now I know I was probably experiencing "culture shock." Culture shock usually refers to a feeling of disorientation or confusion resulting from a person's sudden exposure to an unfamiliar culture, way of life, or set of attitudes.[89] To put it in layman's terms, I was socially, emotionally, and psychologically uncomfortable. I recall instances where female students would clutch their purses while in the elevator with me. I also recall an instance where one of my professors asked me, "Why did you wear 'Hip-Hop clothes.'" I had no clue what he was referring to at the time. I literally thought to myself, "Hip-Hop clothes? What in the world is that?" Then, there was that one time when a couple of my dormmates asked me to join them at a party

---

[89] Ward, C., Bochner, S., & Furnham, A. (2001). *The psychology of culture shock* (2nd ed.). Routledge.

off campus. Yet, when I arrived at the party, they were waiting outside for me. They said, "Hey JT, you probably should not go in because there are some people dressed up in 'blackface.'" I had no clue what "blackface" was at that time in my life. Again, keep in mind that I grew up in a predominantly Black community with individuals who shared a common socioeconomic background and many of the same cultural norms and values. To some extent, my upbringing sheltered me from the realization of a multicultural world beyond my community.

Experiences From a PWI to an HBCU

As a young adult, I did not realize the complexities and nuances associated with cultural expressions among and within racial groups. After my sophomore year at CNU, I decided to transfer to Norfolk State University (NSU), which was a Historically Black College and University (HBCU). This move provided me with a plethora of new cultural experiences. The biggest cultural revelation that I received while at NSU was the fact that "color" and "culture" are two different things. Meaning just because two people may share the same racial identity does not mean they share the same cultural identity. For example, I met numerous African students on NSU's campus who looked just like me, but we did not share the same clothing styles, musical interests, or customs. In many cases, we did not share the same language or accents. We were Black, but our cultures were diverse.

By unpacking my story, I have tried to illustrate and model what engaging in critical self-reflection might look like. As I reflected on my upbringing, I became aware of the role my family and other key individuals played in helping me develop my values. As I reflected on the fact that the K-12 schools I attended as a child were homogenous in terms of racial and socioeconomic diversity, I realized that I was sheltered from multicultural experiences. My experiences can be described as "bi-cultural" at best, meaning my cultural experiences were limited to just two different cultures. This was true during my K-12 experiences as well as my experiences in college. Through my experiences at a predominantly White institution of higher education and an HBCU, I learned that race and culture are not synonyms. By engaging in critical self-reflection and exploring the key experiences that have shaped my life, I can now understand why I have readily embraced culturally responsive approaches to teaching and learning. My lived experiences cultivated my curiosity for this work.

My Experiences as an Educator

While my upbringing and experiences at college greatly impacted my values and beliefs, nothing influenced my approach to teaching and learning more than working in the classroom as a teacher. I honed my pedagogical skills during my time serving as a high school special education teacher working in the inclusion setting. For over 10 years, I served as a co-teacher in English, Biology, Earth Science, and Algebra classes. The student demographics at my school were the most diverse in our district. For example, we had the highest percentage of African American and Hispanic students in the district. As a special educator, I was responsible for helping a caseload of around 17 boys experience academic and behavioral success. The majority of these young men on my caseload identified as African American, Hispanic, and Bi-racial. While they came from different backgrounds and embraced different cultural values, they shared a common story.

Each student on my caseload was found eligible to receive special education services under the Individuals with Disabilities Education Act (IDEA) categories of specific learning disabilities or emotional disabilities. Most of them had been receiving special education services since elementary school. In addition, each of these students was deemed as "at-risk" of dropping out due to historically underperforming in the academic setting. Although my students were viewed by most educators in my school as having "behavioral issues," I always referred to them as "young scholars." I knew that if I was going to have any success in terms of increasing their academic performance, I would have to help them see the genius that lay dormant within them. Therefore, I was on a mission to cultivate their untapped potential.

During my time in the classroom, I became a respected and recognized educator. I won Teacher of the Year as a high school educator and City-Wide Teacher of the Year for my school district, and I was selected by the Association of Supervision and Curriculum Development (ASCD) as an Emerging Leader (Class of 2019). I was also presenting at local and national conferences on the effectiveness of building relationships with students and employing culturally responsive approaches for meeting the needs of diverse students. By this time, many educational leaders from across the nation were seeking my assistance to help them move their schools toward becoming culturally responsive.

No doubt, I was on a mission to help other educators successfully improve the academic achievement of diverse learners by employing culturally responsive pedagogies. By working with thousands of educators from different parts of the United States, I developed the belief that many of the academic problems students were having in the learning space were not caused by deficiencies within the student. In fact, in my heart, I believe that the so-called "achievement gaps" are actually gaps in culturally responsive instruction caused by incongruent attitudes and beliefs held by educators concerning diverse students' academic potential. From my perspective, educators tend to over-scaffold and limit students' access to rigorous learning opportunities. These actions are often rooted in implicit beliefs about the academic capability of diverse students. Not to mention, many educators view students' cultures as liabilities and not assets in the academic space.

Students' Cultures as Instructional Tools

It was during my time working as a special educator that I learned the value and importance of connecting with students on a cultural level. I learned that every educator must seek to develop a positive relationship with students in order to learn about their culture. Once knowledge of a student's culture is gained, the goal becomes integrating elements of the student's culture into the learning space. In a sense, knowledge of students' cultures would become the best instructional tool an educator can employ to increase academic performance. However, too many educators fail to recognize the role culture plays in school.

In his book titled *Why Race and Culture Matter in Schools*, Dr. Tyrone Howard (2020) argued that "Culture matters because it shapes all aspects of daily living and activities" (p. 51).[90] If culture shapes all aspects of daily living and attending school is a prevalent aspect of a student's life, then culture must play a critical role in student learning. Hammond (2015) encouraged educators to "Think of culture as software for the brain's hardware" (p. 22).[91] In other words, it is not possible to separate a student's culture from how their brain makes sense of their experiences during the teaching and learning process. Teaching and learning by nature require a cultural connection because culture is the student's tool for making sense of their world. With this understanding in mind, I sought to explore research on educator attitudes, beliefs, and dispositions about culture and cultural diversity. That journey led me to the construct of multicultural consciousness.[92]

---

[90] Howard, T. (2020). *Why race and culture matter in schools: Closing the achievement gap in America's classrooms* (2nd ed.). Teachers College Press.
[91] Hammond, Z. (2015). *Culturally responsive teaching and the brain: Promoting authentic engagement and rigor among culturally and linguistically diverse students.* Corwin.
[92] Dean, S. R. (2014). Collaborative efforts: Raising students' multicultural consciousness through academic affairs and student affairs partnerships. *Georgia Journal of College Student Affairs, 30*(2). https://doi.org/10.20429/gcpa.2014.300209

Multicultural Consciousness: A Prerequisite to Becoming Culturally Responsive

I started studying multicultural consciousness in 2020 at the beginning of my journey as a Ph.D. student at Regent University. By this time in my career as an educator, I had been deeply engaged in the research on culturally responsive education. Yet, deep down in my heart, I believed that the effective application of culturally responsive practices would ultimately be determined by educators' attitudes and beliefs about culturally diverse students. For example, if an educator embraces a deficit mindset about students of color, they will never be persuaded to use a culturally responsive approach with fidelity. This is because educators who ascribe to deficit thinking believe their instruction is not the independent variable in student achievement. They believe academic success is solely based on factors related to the student. This mindset will reject the effective use of culturally responsive teaching because the deficit thinking perspective honestly believes that regardless of how hard one works to teach and engage students of color, the instruction will not have a greater influence on student achievement when compared to students' racial, cultural, socioeconomic, or family characteristics. This is a problematic approach. My experiences working intimately with teachers as a Title 1 Instructional Coach and educational consultant taught me that educators need to explore their attitudes, beliefs, and dispositions toward culturally diverse students prior to attempting to employ culturally responsive practices.

After combing through hundreds of articles exploring research pertaining to educator attitudes and beliefs, I stumbled upon the work of Dr. Shannon R. Dean. Dr. Dean developed a construct she referred to as "multicultural consciousness." According to Dean (2017), "multicultural consciousness represents the first step in acquiring competence and developing skills" (p. 176). While this construct was not developed for the field of education, I believe its focus on helping individuals develop foundational awareness prior to developing skills has utility for the field of education. Dean specifically created a tool for exploring multicultural attitudes and beliefs about diversity. She defined multicultural consciousness as "the awareness of self, the knowledge of difference, and an interpersonal disposition toward diverse individuals" (Dean, 2017, p. 176). As soon as I read the definition for multicultural consciousness, I believed it could serve as a framework to help educators become culturally responsive educators.

Awareness of Self

The first component of multicultural consciousness is *awareness of self*. According to Dean (2017), awareness of self is defined as "acknowledgment and appreciation of one's own cultural heritage and how that influences biases, values, beliefs, and emotional responses to culturally different populations; recognition of one's own limitations regarding competence" (p. 5). In other words, it is essential for educators to be aware and appreciative of their own cultural beliefs and heritage prior to becoming aware of students' cultural beliefs and heritage. Not only does the construct of awareness of self emphasize intrapersonal awareness, but it also places emphasis on acknowledging how one's cultural beliefs and heritage influence biases. Therefore, an educator who possesses an awareness of self will be able to recognize one's limits in terms of developing cultural competence. CREs must be willing to develop an awareness of their own identities and an understanding of how those identities impact students during the teaching and learning process. This is a crucial prerequisite to becoming a CRE.

Knowledge of Difference

The second component of multicultural consciousness is *knowledge of difference*. According to Dean, knowledge of difference is the "acknowledgment of diverse beliefs and values, having specific knowledge about others' cultural heritage and sociopolitical contexts, and familiarity with specific populations" (p. 5). When applied to teaching, educators who have developed knowledge of difference will be more likely to counter the adverse effects of deficit thinking and cultural mismatch that persists when educators misunderstand the cultural knowledge students bring into the academic setting. When educators fail to take cultural differences into consideration, responding appropriately to cultural diversity is impossible. Siwatu et al. (2016) contended that "teachers may lack knowledge of their students' culture and lived experiences" (p. 277).[93] Additionally, Capella-Santana (2003) stated, "the discrepancy between teachers' knowledge of diverse cultures and the cultural/ethnic backgrounds of the students they must teach may hinder the teachers' ability to effectively teach all students" (p. 182).[94] This is precisely why educators must develop knowledge of differences.

---

[93] Siwatu, K.O., Chesnut, S.R., Alejandro, A.Y., & Young, H.A. (2016). Examining preservice teachers' culturally responsive teaching self-efficacy doubts. *The Teacher Educator, 51*(4), 277-296. https://doi.org/10.1080/08878730.2016.1192709

[94] Capella-Santana, N. (2003). Voices of teacher candidates: positive changes in multicultural attitudes and knowledge. *The Journal of Education Research, 96*, 182-189. https://doi.org/10.1080/00220670309598806

Interpersonal Disposition

The third and final component of multicultural consciousness is referred to as *interpersonal disposition* (Dean, 2020, p. 6).[95] According to Dean (2020), interpersonal disposition refers to a person's "willingness to interact with diverse others, develop relationships in which multiple perspectives exist, sustain intergroup friendships, and embrace multiple sources of identity" (p. 6). Developing interpersonal disposition does not mean a person is an expert at interacting with diverse others; it simply means a person is willing to interact with diverse others. Clearly, a willingness to work with diverse students must precede the effective application of culturally responsive practices. This is why I argue that all CREs must foster multicultural consciousness as a prerequisite to applying culturally responsive practices in the school setting.

Unfortunately, I have worked with and coached educators who did not prefer to work with diverse youth. Several educators have explicitly told me that once the school year ended at the Title 1 school in which they worked, they planned on transferring to a school with less cultural diversity. However, their desire to transfer does not

---

[95]Dean, S. R. (2020). Shifting language from multicultural competence to consciousness. *Journal of Student Affairs Research and Practice.* https://myacpa.org/wp-content/uploads/2021/10/Shifting-Language.pdf

mean they were racist; it simply meant they lacked interpersonal disposition toward diversity. Since they struggled to reach and teach students of color, they felt that it would be easier and less challenging to work with a population of less diverse students. This is what happens when educators are asked to employ culturally responsive practices without cultivating an interpersonal disposition toward diversity. I argue that it is the responsibility of teacher preparation programs, school districts, and building-level leaders to help educators of culturally diverse students foster multicultural consciousness prior to asking them to employ culturally responsive teaching practices.

Summary of Step 2: Foster Multicultural Consciousness

As mentioned earlier in the work of Dr. Yolanda Sealy-Ruiz (2022), educators must be able to conduct an "archeology of self," which refers to "a deep excavation and exploration of beliefs, biases, and ideas that shape how we engage in our work" (p. 22).[96] In an attempt to model this for educators, I began this section with a deep excavation of my life. I started by exploring my key experiences during my upbringing. Then, I reflected on my

---

[96] Sealy-Ruiz, Y. (2022). An archaeology of self for our times: Another talk to teachers. *English Journal, 111*(5), 21-26. https://library.ncte.org/journals/EJ/issues/v111-5

experiences in K-12 schools and institutions of higher education. Lastly, I explored my experiences as a paraeducator, special education teacher, Title 1 Instructional Coach, and full-time educational consultant. This process of critical self-examination is a key component of multicultural consciousness.

Remember, multicultural consciousness involves three components: awareness of self, knowledge of difference, and interpersonal disposition toward diversity. I argue that multicultural consciousness is a prerequisite to becoming a CRE. My premise is based on the notion that attitudes and beliefs precede actions. Therefore, before we can ask educators to apply culturally responsive practices in the school system, we must first ensure that educators possess culturally responsive attitudes and beliefs. Fostering multicultural consciousness will allow educators to dispel deficit thinking and low expectations about culturally diverse students. This is necessary to engage in the effective application of culturally responsive teaching practices.

Extension Questions for Educators to Consider:

1. What's your story? Did you have many multicultural experiences during your youth? If yes, what were they?

2. Would you describe your upbringing as predominantly monocultural (meaning, you were primarily surrounded by people who identified with your culture), bi-cultural (meaning, you were mostly surrounded by people from two different cultures), or multicultural (meaning, you were surrounded by individuals from diverse cultural backgrounds)?
3. Were there many diverse students in your elementary, middle, or high school?
4. Did you attend a diverse institution of higher education?
5. How have your experiences as an educator influenced your beliefs about culturally diverse students?
6. Have you ever lived with or spent a significant amount of time with others who were culturally diverse?
7. Where did you gain the knowledge that you possess about diverse students?

Step 3: Apply Culturally Responsive Approaches

Step 3 - Apply Culturally Responsive Approaches

"Students quickly receive the message that they can only be smart when they are not who they are. This, in many ways, is classroom colonialism; and it can only be addressed through a very different approach to teaching and learning."
- CHRISTOPHER EMDIN

Essential Question: How will we know that educators are effectively applying culturally responsive approaches?

Now that we have explored the need to develop historical awareness and foster multicultural consciousness, we can proceed to the effective application of culturally responsive approaches in schools. This is arguably the most critical component of becoming a CRE. Educators need to know when they are actually demonstrating a culturally responsive approach. We need to be able to identify the practices that are, in fact, responsive to the students we serve. Therefore, the goal of this section is to provide observable examples and actions that can serve as "look fors" for educators who desire to identify culturally responsive practices within the school setting.

Before we tackle indicators of culturally responsive approaches and practices in the school context, I believe it necessary to review what we mean when we use the phrase "culturally responsive." According to Howard (2020), culturally responsive pedagogical approaches are rooted in the following five key principles: [97]

1. "The eradication of deficit-based ideologies about culturally diverse students.
2. The disruption of the idea that Eurocentric or middle-class forms of discourse, knowledge, language, culture, and historical interpretations are normative.
3. A critical consciousness and sociopolitical awareness that reflects an ongoing commitment to challenge injustice and disrupt inequities and oppression of any group of people.
4. An authentic and culturally informed notion of *care* for students, wherein their academic, social, emotional, psychological, and cultural well-being is adhered to.
5. A recognition of the complexity of culture, in which educators allow students to use their personal culture to enhance their quest for educational excellence" (p. 67).[98]

---

[97] Howard, T. (2020). *Why race and culture matter in schools: Closing the achievement gap in America's classrooms* (2nd ed.). Teachers College Press.
[98] Ibid.

That is *NOT* Culturally Responsive!

While it is important to develop an ability to identify culturally responsive approaches, it might be equally beneficial to understand when approaches and practices are NOT culturally responsive. For example, when deficit narratives about students, their families, or their communities are perpetuated in schools, we can conclude that this behavior is not aligned with the principles of culturally responsive approaches. When educators disregard the many ways that culturally diverse students display brilliance because Eurocentric values and middle-class ideas for evaluating intelligence are considered normative, we can conclude that this practice is not culturally responsive. Additionally, anytime educators are content with turning a blind eye to visible injustice and inequity in schools, we can conclude that this behavior is not aligned with being culturally responsive.

Similarly, we can identify educators who are not culturally responsive by their attitudes, beliefs, and dispositions about culturally diverse students. When educators confuse caring for diverse students with over-scaffolding or having pity on them because they are minoritized, these educators are not being culturally responsive. Diverse students do not need "academic saviors;" instead, they need educators who believe in their brilliance and hold them to high expectations. Furthermore, when educators intentionally or unintentionally make students feel that they must be something other than themselves in the instructional environment, they are not being culturally responsive. Each child should feel free enough to unapologetically be themselves. No child should internalize the belief that "I must leave my culture at the door when I enter the school or class if I desire to be successful in this space."

Creating a Culturally Responsive School Culture

CREs are committed to immersing students in a culturally responsive schooling experience. Immediately upon entering a school building, students should feel embraced by a school culture that can be described as responsive to diverse students. In other words, the atmosphere of the school should communicate the following to each learner: *"We see you, we appreciate you, we welcome you, you are valued here, and this is your space too."* Every student should experience a school culture that can be described as love personified. This means every student should feel the warmth of acceptance and belonging when they enter the school. This is the type of school culture that educators should strive to create for students. So, how do we do this work? How can educators create a culturally responsive school culture? How can educators demonstrate their commitment to becoming culturally responsive? I believe the quickest way to identify whether or not a school is applying culturally responsive approaches is to employ the "**V-Framework**." The V-Framework will allow educators to identify culturally responsive *vision*, *values*, and *visible evidence* within the school context. Please see the diagram illustrating the "V-Framework."

"V-Framework"
A Guide for Evaluating Culturally Responsiveness in Schools

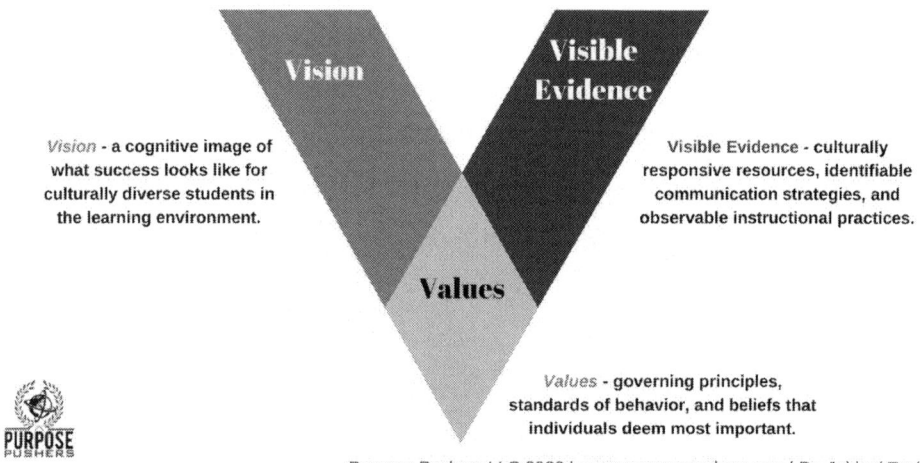

Vision

Visible Evidence

Vision - a cognitive image of what success looks like for culturally diverse students in the learning environment.

Visible Evidence - culturally responsive resources, identifiable communication strategies, and observable instructional practices.

Values

Values - governing principles, standards of behavior, and beliefs that individuals deem most important.

Purpose Pushers LLC 2023 | www.purposepushers.com | Dr. Jahkari Taylor

It All Starts with **Vision**

Educators cannot apply a culturally responsive approach if they lack a clear vision for what a culturally responsive approach should look like in their context. Therefore, everything starts with a vision for a culturally responsive approach to education. Questions that need consideration include the following: Has the superintendent, principal, or site leader articulated a clear vision for the integration of culturally responsive approaches? Have the educators in the space defined what a culturally responsive school culture looks like? Do teachers have a clear vision of what culturally responsive practices look like in the classroom setting? Inquiring about the presence or absence of a culturally responsive vision is the essential first step in the process of creating a culturally responsive school culture.

The term *vision* is not as popular in education as it is in the field of business. In business, vision can refer to "a cognitive image of a desired future state" (Kantabutra et al., 2008, p.127).[99] According to Collins and Porras (1996), vision is the core ideology that defines the enduring character of an organization and serves as the glue that holds the organization together.[100] Leaders in the field of business usually create a statement to articulate their vision to ensure that everyone understands the core

---

[99] Kantabutra, S. (2010). What do we know about vision. Leading organizations: perspectives for a new era. *The Journal of Applied Business Research, 24*(2), 127-138. https://doi.org/10.19030/jabr.v24i2.1359
[100] Collins, J. C., & Porras, J. I. (1996). Building your company's vision. *Harvard business review, 74*(5), 65. https://www.cin.ufpe.br/~genesis/docpublicacoes/visao.pdf

purpose of the organization. This *vision statement* usually provides the rationale for why the organization exists.

Similar to leaders in the field of business who use their vision to communicate what they stand for, what they desire to accomplish, and what they desire to create within the context of the organization, I argue that educational leaders must be able to conceive and articulate a culturally responsive vision of what success looks like for culturally diverse students in the academic space. Educational leaders should be able to point to a clear vision of what culturally responsive approaches should look like in their specific context. Without a clear vision of what culturally responsive approaches look like in the school and classroom setting, educators will have unclear expectations about what it means to be a CRE. Thus, educational leaders who desire to see the successful application of culturally responsive approaches in the learning environment should draft a vision statement that can guide their actions and the actions of other educators in the academic setting.

Let me be clear; it is the responsibility of leadership to create and articulate a culturally responsive vision statement for the district or school. As leadership guru John Maxwell stated in his book, *The 21 Irrefutable Laws of Leadership*, "Everything rises and falls on leadership" (p.

267).[101] In the same way, a school's ability to uphold and apply the principles and practices associated with culturally responsive education will be determined by the leader's vision of what culturally responsive approaches entail. To develop a culturally responsive vision statement, leaders must be able to answer the following questions:
- What will culturally responsive approaches look like in our school?
- How do we define a culturally responsive school culture?
- What are the key characteristics of a culturally responsive teacher in our school?
- What are the key characteristics of a culturally responsive classroom in our school?
- How will our professional development plan align with our expectations for culturally responsive educators in our school?

Once leaders are able to answer these questions, they will be one step closer to casting a compelling vision that describes what is meant by "being culturally responsive" in the learning environment. As educational leaders conceive and articulate a culturally responsive vision of what success should look like for diverse students in the school, teachers will be able to align their actions

---

[101] Maxwell, J. (2007). *The 21 irrefutable laws of leadership.* Harper Collins Leadership.

with the leader's vision. This is why a culturally responsive vision is necessary to create a culturally responsive school culture. The leader's vision ultimately becomes the foundational tool used to paint a clear picture of the preferred reality, namely what a culturally responsive school or classroom looks like.

Examples of a Culturally Responsive Vision Statement

- At Purpose Pushers Elementary School, we nurture cultural diversity by employing diverse instructional practices to ensure each child has access to rigorous learning opportunities in a warm, safe, and inclusive environment.
- At Purpose Pushers Middle School, we recognize diversity as a strength and employ culturally responsive approaches to increase the academic achievement of each student.
- At Purpose Pushers High School, we engage students in a culturally sensitive and affirming curriculum designed to equip them with the skills needed to make a global impact in a diverse world.

Values Drive the Vision

Once we have evaluated the presence or absence of a culturally responsive vision, we can begin to look for culturally responsive values. Questions may include: What governing expectations should be standardized for culturally diverse learners? What values must every educator be expected to embrace to demonstrate a commitment to culturally responsive practices? In the most general sense, values refer to the governing principles, standards of behavior, and beliefs that individuals deem most important.[102] Most organizations communicate their values to staff in an attempt to drive the organization's behavior toward accomplishing the organizational vision. When organizations fail to establish values, each individual within the organization embraces their own individual value system.[103] This can lead to problems such as confusion and division among staff. For example, a 6th grade teacher in "classroom A" may disagree with the application of culturally responsive practices in "classroom B." If no one can refer to a clear vision and clear values that articulate exactly how culturally responsive practices should manifest in the school, this disagreement will most likely be fueled by a subjective understanding of what constitutes culturally responsive practices in school, which can lead to larger issues. Needless to say, a lack of clear values can create unnecessary barriers to accomplishing the vision.

Therefore, it is imperative for clear values to be established, communicated, and upheld. In the context of school, it is beneficial for educators to establish and

---

[102] Bell, W. F. (n.d.). *The impact of policies on organizational values and culture.* http://isme.tamu.edu/JSCOPE99/Bell99.html
[103] Ibid.

promote culturally responsive values. These values should be used to govern communication and behavior concerning culturally responsive practices. Here are a few examples of culturally responsive values and their possible impact on organizational behavior:

Example - Culturally Responsive Values Chart

Values	Possible Impact on Organizational Behavior
Empathy	By establishing empathy as a key value in the school or classroom setting, educators may be more likely to demonstrate sensitivity and understanding toward culturally diverse students.
Student-Centered	By establishing student-centered as a key value in the school or classroom setting, educators may be more likely to consider the need to center each student's voice, identity, and interests when creating learning experiences.
Respect	By establishing respect as a key value in the school or classroom setting, educators may be more likely to demonstrate and promote respect for cultural differences in the learning environment.
Culturally-Responsive	By establishing culturally-responsive as a key value in the school or classroom setting, educators may be more likely to recognize the importance of including students' culture in all areas of the learning environment

The goal of the aforementioned values chart is not to provide an exhaustive list of culturally responsive values but to provide an example of how culturally responsive values can be used to drive organizational behavior. Without clear values rooted in a vision for a culturally responsive school culture, many educators may embrace values that are not necessarily conducive for the effective application of culturally responsive approaches in the school setting. This occurs not because educators do not desire to employ best practices for engaging culturally diverse students but because a general misunderstanding of what culturally responsive values look like in the educational space will be maintained when clarity is lacking. For this reason, educational leaders must provide clarity of values. Once a clear vision and clear values are provided for educators, educational leaders can move to the final component of the V-Framework: visible evidence.

Provide Visible Evidence - "The Culturally Responsive Observation A.R.C."

Visible evidence refers to observable and identifiable culturally responsive practices within the school context. The language of visible evidence provides the answer to the essential question at the beginning of this section: How will educators know when they are effectively applying culturally responsive approaches? The answer is when evidence of culturally responsive approaches is visible in the learning environment. When students, teachers, leaders, counselors, parents, and other key members of the school community can see and attest to the visibility of culturally responsive approaches in the school, we have effectively applied culturally responsive practices. In other words, visible evidence is the only appropriate indicator.

To assist with identifying visible evidence of culturally responsive practices, I have developed *The A.R.C. Framework*. "ARC" is an acronym that stands for *atmosphere*, *resources*, and *communication*. The A.R.C. Framework is designed to assist educators in their pursuit of conceptualizing areas where visible evidence of culturally responsive practices must be indicated. The three key areas of the A.R.C. include the school or classroom **atmosphere**, the instructional **resources** available to students, and the **communication** styles and techniques used by staff when delivering instruction. Let's explore the A.R.C. Framework in greater detail. *(To download a personal copy of the A.R.C. Frameworks, utilize the QR code in the back of this book.)*

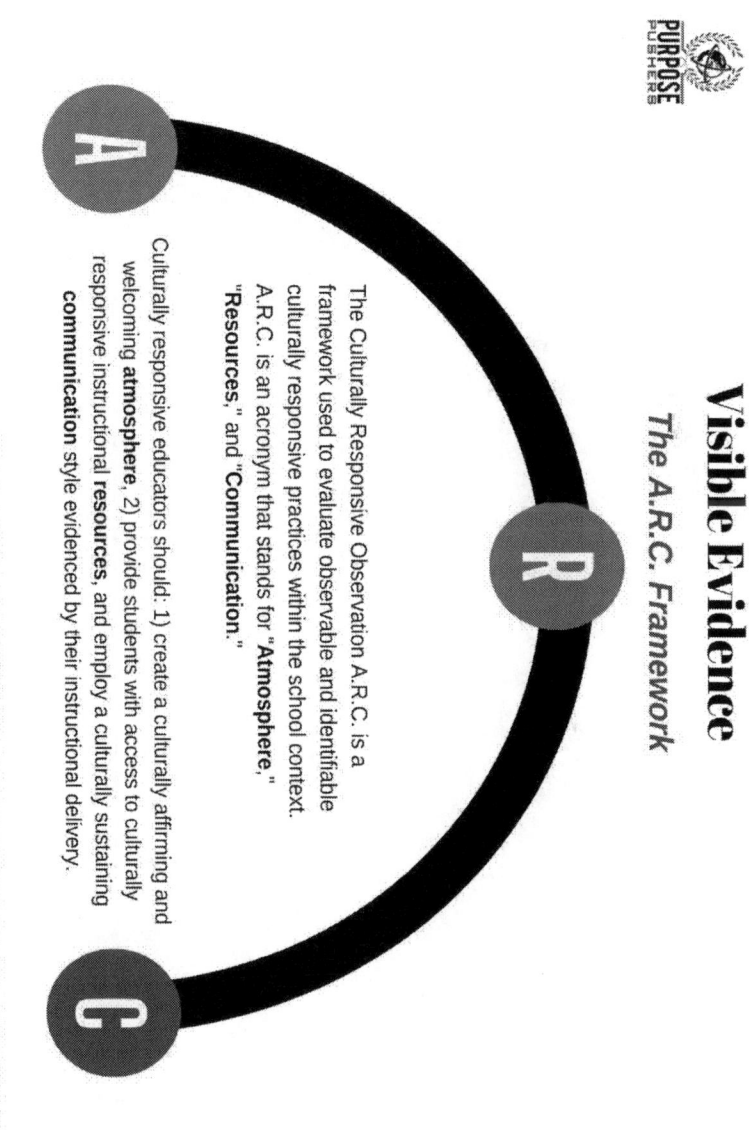

Visible Evidence
The A.R.C. Framework

The Culturally Responsive Observation A.R.C. is a framework used to evaluate observable and identifiable culturally responsive practices within the school context. A.R.C. is an acronym that stands for "**Atmosphere**," "**Resources**," and "**Communication**."

Culturally responsive educators should: 1) create a culturally affirming and welcoming **atmosphere**, 2) provide students with access to culturally responsive instructional **resources**, and employ a culturally sustaining **communication** style evidenced by their instructional delivery.

Visible Evidence

The A.R.C. Framework - Indicator Checklist (IC)

A

Visible evidence and observable indicators of a culturally responsive **atmosphere** may include:

- ☐ Posters, wall hangings, and decorations that indicate cultural diversity is valued.
- ☐ Images of heroes, holidays, and historical events illustrating an appreciation for cultural diversity is apparent within the school or classroom (Gay, 2018).

R

Visible evidence and observable indicators of culturally responsive **resources** may include:

- ☐ Increased access to culturally and historically responsive reading materials - i.e., books, poetry, digital texts, blogs, social media posts, journals, etc. (Muhammad, 2020).
- ☐ Curricula containing empowering images that represent the strengths of diverse people rather than their perceived flaws or deficiencies (Bryan-Gooden, Hester, & Peoples, 2019).

C

Visible evidence and observable indicators of a culturally responsive **communication** style may include:

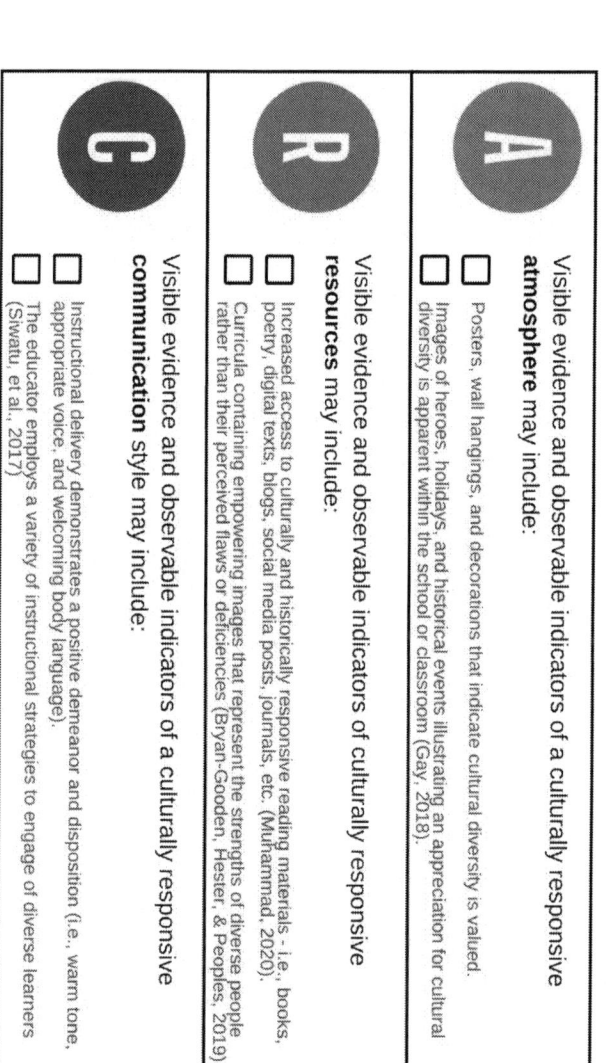

- ☐ Instructional delivery demonstrates a positive demeanor and disposition (i.e., warm tone, appropriate voice, and welcoming body language).
- ☐ The educator employs a variety of instructional strategies to engage of diverse learners (Siwatu, et al., 2017)

Purpose Pushers LLC 2023 | www.purposepushers.com | Dr. Jahkari Taylor

Atmosphere - Culturally Responsive Learning Atmosphere

To evaluate visible evidence in the school or classroom atmosphere, one can ask the following questions: How does it feel to be a student in this school? Do you feel welcomed, affirmed, and valued in school? Does the classroom atmosphere feel warm, friendly, and inviting? Would you describe most adults in this school as caring and encouraging? While evaluating the school or classroom atmosphere might initially seem to be abstract or nebulous, a culturally responsive atmosphere is not difficult to assess. One strategy could be employing a survey to students, staff, or parents/families. The survey does not have to be long and drawn out. It could simply ask a variation of questions: How does it feel to be a student in this school? Do you see posters, wall hangings, and decorations around the school that demonstrate contributions from diverse people? Have you noticed any images and pictures of heroes, scientists, and leaders from diverse backgrounds on the bulletin boards? These questions can provide clues to help us better understand the atmosphere and climate of a school.

As an educational consultant, I am frequently invited to help educational leaders move their schools in the direction of becoming culturally responsive. When the opportunity presents itself, the first thing I do is request a tour of the school site. During this tour, I conducted a personal, culturally responsive school audit. Upon entry into the school, I begin making observations and jotting down anecdotal notes. I specifically look for posters, wall hangings, and decorations that would indicate that cultural diversity is valued in the space. I also look for samples of students' work which, for me, tend to communicate that this is a student space. I always use the analogy of a person's home to help others understand why posting student work samples is important. For example, when I enter my house, I see images of myself, my family, and personal items that I consider to be valuable. In the same way, a student-centered environment should reflect elements created by students. Students should see their work samples posted. In addition, students should see items that they value in the learning environment. This communicates a sense of "this is your space" to students.

Along with student work samples and other references that are valuable to students, I look for visible evidence that would indicate that the atmosphere is intentionally designed to make students of color feel empowered and capable. There is a plethora of ways to accomplish this task. I have already named a few strategies, but I will also add depicting images and artifacts of culturally diverse brilliance. For example, every Math class should have culturally diverse mathematicians posterized around the room, every Science class should expose students to images of culturally diverse scientists, and every English Language Arts class should introduce students to culturally diverse authors. By doing this, minoritized students will begin to internalize the brilliance they see in individuals who look like them. In addition, White students will become more aware of the contributions of people from diverse cultural backgrounds. This can be culturally empowering and enlightening for all students. In the introduction, I explained how Carlos changed my pedagogy by asking, "Mr. Taylor, are there any Hispanic scientists? Then, why don't we learn about them." As in Carlos' case, some children need to be exposed to brilliant individuals who look like them and identify with their cultural backgrounds.

Utilizing posters, images, and other wall hangings to elevate culturally diverse brilliance is one powerful way to provide visible evidence of a school or classroom atmosphere that is at least attempting to be culturally affirming. This is something that can be quickly evaluated using a checklist or observation tool.

Resources - Culturally Responsive Instructional Resources and Materials

Along with providing visible evidence of a culturally affirming atmosphere, CRE must also provide students with access to culturally responsive resources. In her book

Cultivating Genius: An Equity Framework for Culturally and Historically Responsive Literacy, Dr. Gholdy Muhammad (2020) argued that students should be exposed to books and other literary texts that motivate them to engage in social action with a determined attitude to change their world for the better. Muhammad believes every child should have access to culturally and historically responsive literature. Since teachers have the power to be gatekeepers in terms of determining what resources students have access to, it is essential for every educator to become culturally responsive.

The reality is some students may never gain access to empowering literature during their PreK-12 experience if educators refuse to intentionally expose them to culturally responsive resources and instructional materials. To help educators evaluate whether students have access to culturally responsive curricula in English Language Arts classrooms, the New York University Metropolitan Center for Research on Equity and the Transformation of Schools (NYU Metro Center) created a "Culturally Responsive Curriculum Scorecard" that is designed to evaluate the extent to which a school's English Language Arts curriculum is culturally responsive.[104] The NYU Metro Center utilized multicultural rubrics, anti-bias

---

[104] Bryan-Gooden, J., Hester, M., & Peoples, L. Q. (2019*). Culturally responsive curriculum scorecard.* Metropolitan Center for Research on Equity and the Transformation of Schools, New York University.

rubrics, textbook rubrics, and a host of other frameworks to develop this comprehensive tool. The Culturally Responsive Curriculum Scorecard allows individuals to tally the number of diverse characters depicted in the available books and reading resources within the classroom. Additionally, it allows evaluators to tally the number of diverse authors reflected in the reading materials. Then, it goes further by reviewing how diverse characters in the reading materials are portrayed. Do the characters fit into a stereotypical narrative? Do the resources "communicate negativity or hostility toward people of marginalized backgrounds through verbal or nonverbal insults, slights or snubs?"[105] These critical questions about the instructional materials made available to culturally diverse students can be answered by utilizing the Culturally Responsive Curriculum Scorecard.

CREs seek to provide diverse students access to culturally responsive books, worksheets, journal prompts, and other instructional materials. The goal is to use culturally responsive resources to help young people develop an appreciation for cultural diversity and to empower culturally diverse young people. Culturally responsive resources have always been a staple in U.S. schools. Yet, it is believed that these resources have been "most responsive to only one group of students—U.S.-

---

[105] Ibid, p. 11.

born, middle-class, English-speaking, White students" (Howard, 2020, p.68).[106] In other words, instructional resources have always been empowering to students. However, it is the goal of CREs to ensure that culturally diverse students also have access to empowering resources and instructional materials.

Communication - Culturally Responsive Communication and Instructional Delivery

Creating a culturally affirming atmosphere is necessary, and providing students with access to culturally responsive instructional materials is commendable, but the most important component in education still revolves around **communication**. How should a CRE engage students in a dialogue that leads to learning? How should instructional concepts be communicated to culturally diverse students? What if an educator creates a culturally affirming atmosphere and provides students with culturally responsive resources but fails to engage students in dynamic, culturally affirming instruction? What if the communication of key concepts falls flat due to a boring, unenthusiastic instructional delivery? I argue that student

---

[106] Howard, T. (2020). *Why race and culture matter in schools: Closing the achievement gap in America's classrooms* (2nd ed.). Teachers College Press.

learning will always be heavily impacted by how educators communicate in the instructional setting.

Culturally responsive practices are not just about the atmosphere and resources available but also about instructional delivery. In her book titled, *Culturally Responsive Teaching & the Brain: Promoting Authentic Engagement and Rigor Among Culturally and Linguistically Diverse Students*, Zaretta Hammond (2015) argued that culturally responsive teaching is "more than a motivational tool... it is a serious and powerful tool for accelerating student learning" (p.3). Therefore, to become a CRE, one must commit to perpetual improvement as it relates to pedagogy (the art and science of teaching). Gloria Ladson-Billings, whom I consider to be the mother of culturally responsive approaches, explained that culturally responsive pedagogy (CRP) is an empowering pedagogy that rests on three propositions: "(1) students must experience academic success; (2) students must develop and/or maintain cultural competence; and (3) students must develop a critical consciousness through which they challenge the status quo of the current social order" (1995, p. 160).[107] Also, according to Howard (2020), CRP

> embodies a professional, political, cultural, ethical, and ideological disposition that supersedes mundane

---

[107] Ladson-Billings, G. (1995). But that's just good teaching! The case for culturally relevant pedagogy. *Theory into Practice, 34*(3), 159-165. https://doi.org/10.1080/00405849509543675

teaching acts; it is centered in fundamental beliefs about teaching, learning, students, their families, and their communities, and an unyielding commitment to see student success become less rhetoric and more of a reality. (p. 65)[108]

Ladson-Billings (2009) noted that CRP should "empower students intellectually, socially, emotionally, and politically using cultural referents to impart knowledge, skills, and attitudes" (p. 16).[109] Therefore, CRE must use their words to speak life into culturally diverse students in such a way that these students are empowered to succeed at a high academic level. Communication should always be perceived by students as caring, and it should also contribute to students' emotional wholeness and confidence in the academic space. If communicating with diverse students does not help them to reveal their brilliance to the world, it is insufficient at best. They deserve culturally responsive communication that brings out the best in them. (*For more specific communication strategies, review the "Cultural Considerations When Implementing CRCM" subheading in Section 1 of this book.*)

---

[108] Howard, T. (2020). Why race and culture matter in schools: *Closing the achievement gap in America's classrooms* (2nd ed.). Teachers College Press.
[109] Ladson-Billings, G. (2009). *The dreamkeepers: Successful teachers of African American children* (2nd ed). Jossey Bass.

Culturally Responsive Approaches in Action: Christian Preachers

While it is true that many teachers apply culturally responsive instructional practices in classrooms across the nation, I have also found some of the most effective examples of CREs outside of the school context. In fact, I have witnessed countless Christian preachers utilizing culturally responsive approaches to effectively engage diverse audiences within the context of the church. Although they may not label their communication techniques as culturally responsive, these preachers model the principles of culturally responsive approaches. Like educators employing culturally responsive approaches in the classroom setting, Christian preachers often communicate with a dynamic instructional delivery to increase engagement. Using microphones to amplify their voices, they use vocabulary terms and stories that are familiar with their audience's lived experiences to activate and build upon prior knowledge. This preaching technique is referred to as "bridge-building" (p.3). [110] Bridge-building refers to connecting biblical content to pressing cultural issues within the modern sociopolitical context while valuing diverse cultural groups within church congregations. According to Kim (2017), "Preachers

---

[110] Kim, M. D. (2017). *Preaching with cultural intelligence: Understanding the people who hear our sermons.* Baker Academic.

survey a checkerboard of eclectic people sitting in the pews, trying to make sense of how they can integrate the disparate pieces of their hearers' lives into a clear, contextualized, and unified message. This bridge-building exercise in preaching warrants cultural intelligence" (p. 3).[111]

Bridge-building is indeed a culturally responsive approach to teaching and learning. One of the best bridge-building preachers I have heard of is Dr. Tony Evans, the senior pastor of Oak Cliff Bible Fellowship in Dallas, Texas. In a mini-sermon titled "Football and Faith with Tony Evans," Dr. Evans shared a personal story from his youth that took place on a football field. He explained that he had sustained a broken leg while playing with his friends. While he acknowledged the painful and unfortunate event, he also mentioned a few valuable lessons he learned from that situation. Dr. Evans noted that his experience with a broken leg proved to him that it is possible for brokenness to be completely healed. He stated, "Our nation is broken, our communities are broken, families are broken, lives are broken, but God is able to reset breaks and get you back on your feet."[112]

Dr. Evans used the analogy of football to set the stage for a theological connection. I believe he chose

---
[111] Ibid., p.3.
[112] Evans, T. (2013). *Football and faith with Tony Evans*. YouTube. https://www.youtube.com/watch?v=VBWEQQMk1Ig

football because it is likely a popular sport among members of his congregation. In essence, his football story is his tool to tap into the cultural competence that his audience is bringing into the space. It is merely the "bridge" to help his audience better understand a theological truth. From an instructional perspective, Dr. Evans used the football analogy as the anticipatory set that activated prior knowledge and prepared his audience for direct and explicit theological instruction. Once his audience was engaged in his football story, he connected his experience with a broken leg to the "brokenness" that characterizes the lived experiences of many Americans. He then offered an encouraging conclusion to teach a theological truth that would hopefully stimulate reflection and provoke action.

    Culturally responsive approaches within the context of a classroom should follow a similar format. First, CREs should develop an understanding of students' interests, aspirations, and lived experiences. Then, the knowledge about students should be integrated into the curriculum. Once the bridge is built between the students' cultural competence and the curricular materials, CREs should employ communication techniques and vocabulary terms that are congruent with students' cultural backgrounds. In other words, what one teaches is never as important as how one teaches. Culturally responsive instruction can occur in any subject. It is all about how content is packaged and presented to culturally diverse students. The goal is always to "empower students intellectually, socially, emotionally, and politically using cultural referents to impart knowledge, skills, and attitudes" (Ladson-Billings, 2009, p. 20).[113]

---

[113] Ladson-Billings, G. (2009). *The dreamkeepers: Successful teachers of African American children* (2nd ed). Jossey Bass.

Summary of Step 3: Applying Culturally Responsive Approaches

If the goal is to apply culturally responsive practices to increase the academic achievement of diverse learners, educators must have a clear vision of what culturally responsive practices will look like in the school setting. In the ideal world, a culturally responsive school vision must start with school leaders. This is why culturally responsive school leaders are paramount to the work of becoming CREs. Johnson (2014) stated, "culturally responsive leadership, derived from the concept of culturally responsive pedagogy, incorporates those leadership philosophies, practices, and policies that create inclusive schooling environments for students and families from ethnically and culturally diverse backgrounds" (p.145).[114]

Every school requires culturally responsive leaders who possess the ability to create an environment where CREs can thrive while creating thriving conditions for diverse students. These culturally responsive leaders must conceive and communicate a compelling vision for a caring and culturally responsive school community. By articulating a clear vision and core values (or belief statements to hold everyone in the organization accountable), the school will

---

[114] Johnson, L. (2014). Culturally responsive leadership for community empowerment. *Multicultural Education Review, 6*(2), 145-170. http://dx.doi.org/10.14328/MER.2014.09.30.145

position itself to apply culturally responsive approaches across the school community. Once leaders model this step, staff can follow their lead by embracing culturally responsive values or beliefs that will serve as guiding principles, norms, and standards within the instructional setting.

To ensure that educators in the school are effectively applying culturally responsive approaches, I recommend utilizing the *V-Framework*, *The Culturally Responsive Values Chart*, and the *A.R.C. Framework* as supplemental aids. These frameworks and diagrams may be able to assist leaders, teachers, and other educators who are seeking to evaluate the effective application of culturally responsive practices in schools. I concluded Step 3 by providing an example of culturally responsive approaches being applied outside of the school context. This example is used to help educators understand the practical utility of culturally responsive approaches to reach diverse audiences. For those who need more examples of culturally responsive practices, I have listed seven additional instructional strategies below:

1. **Hold students to high academic expectations.**
2. **Explicitly teach students to be respectful of cultural differences.**
    a. This can be done through writing prompts, book talks, videos, classroom values, reviewing PBIS matrices, etc.

3. **Administer biographical and autobiographical writing assignments.**
    a. Teachers can use this approach to literacy instruction to help students build cultural competence and diversify their knowledge base. In addition, teachers can help students strengthen their intrapersonal awareness skills while honing their writing skills. These assignments can also provide educators with insight and background information about students' upbringing, recreational interests outside of school, aspirations and post-secondary goals, languages spoken at home, favorite food, musical interests, and much more.[115]
4. **Use insight from autobiographical assignments to plan culturally responsive lessons.**
5. **Activate students' prior knowledge.**
    a. Gay (2018) stated, "Begin teaching culturally diverse students of color using what they already know" (p.245).[116]
6. **Employ academic learning games.**
    a. Teachers must recognize that many students identify with "gaming culture." Therefore, computer games, board games, and even card

---

[115] Herrera, S. (2010). *Biography-driven culturally responsive teaching.* Teachers College Press.
[116] Gay, G. (2018). *Culturally responsive teaching.* Teachers College Press.

games should be considered in the academic space. For example, a simple card game can easily be used to help elementary students strengthen their number sense and mathematical computation skills (addition and subtraction).
7. **Use current events to help students develop sociopolitical awareness and empathy.**[117]
    a. Secondary educators can use cooperative grouping to help students collaborate to address issues that might impact their communities.

Extension Questions for Educators to Consider:

1. Does my school have a vision for culturally responsive practices? How do I know?
2. Has my school developed culturally responsive values to guide organizational behavior? Have I solidified culturally responsive values that will guide my classroom culture?
3. Can I point to any observable or identifiable culturally responsive practices in my school?
4. Have we created an atmosphere in our school that is warm, affirming, and empowering for culturally diverse students?

---

[117] Ladson-Billings, G. (2009). *The dreamkeepers: Successful teachers of African American children* (2nd ed). Jossey Bass.

5. Do culturally diverse students have access to culturally and historically responsive resources and instructional materials?
6. Are educators committed to providing students with a dynamic and engaging instructional delivery that empowers them to reveal their brilliance to the world?
7. If I were a culturally diverse student in my current school or district, would I be satisfied with the education being afforded?

Step 4: Prioritize Family and Community Engagement

Step 4 - Prioritize Family and Community Engagement

"When beginning teachers come into minority communities, many are unable to understand the students' home language, social interaction patterns, histories, and cultures. Thus, they cannot truly educate the students. Their perceptions of deficiency and competence are socially and culturally constructed. Without greater exposure to the students' culture teachers lack the tools with which to make sense of much that transpires in the classroom."[118]
- GLORIA LADSON-BILLINGS

Essential Question: Can educators be culturally responsive while neglecting family and community engagement?

For decades, researchers have recognized the positive impact parent, family, and community engagement in school has on student success.[119] The problem is many schools serving Black and Brown students fail to

---

[118] Ladson-Billings, G. (2009). *The dreamkeepers: successful teachers of African American children* (2nd ed). Jossey Bass.

[119] Bryan, J., & Henry, L. (2008). Strengths-based partnerships: A school-family-community partnership approach to empowering students. *Professional School Counseling, 12*(2), 149-156. http://dx.doi.org/10.5330/PSC.n.2010-12.149

Gobby, B., & Niesche, R. (2019). Community empowerment? School autonomy, school boards and depoliticizing governance. *Australian Educational Researcher; Dordrecht, 46*(3), 565-582. http://doi.org/10.1007/s13384-019-00303-9

successfully nurture family and community engagement.[120] For this reason, it is not uncommon for parents and families from historically marginalized communities to feel unwelcomed, uninvited, and unwanted in the context of schools. Obviously, this historical disconnect between schools and the communities they serve does not align with the values of CREs. So, the question is, how can schools prioritize family and community engagement in a culturally responsive way? What must schools do to close the gap dividing schools and communities?

In response to the historical disconnect between schools and communities, Dr. Muhammad Khalifa (2018) argued for culturally responsive school leadership (CRSL). From Khalifa's perspective, a paradigm shift in educational leadership must occur. Principals must not only strive to be instructional leaders, but they must also see themselves as community leaders. Khalifa (2018) believed leaders must "engage communities in empowering and humanizing ways" (p. 12).[121] He stated, "Principals must lead schools with community perspectives at the center of their leadership behaviors" (Khalifa, 2018, p.11).[122] Therefore,

---

[120] Green, E. M. (2021). *Family and community engagement: The role of parent, school and community involvement in the academic achievement of African American students in elementary school* (Publication No. 28316338). [Doctoral dissertation, Northcentral University]. ProQuest Dissertations & Theses Global.
[121] Khalifa, M. (2018). *Culturally responsive school leadership.* Harvard Education Press.
[122] Ibid. p.11.

he encourages leaders to engage in the following actions in their attempt to prioritize family and community engagement:

- Engage in critical self-reflection to evaluate how schools may have historically reproduced or perpetuated inequities in diverse communities.
- Encourage teachers and staff to establish positive rapport and build trusting relationships with parents and families.
- Create opportunities to amplify the voices of parents and families (i.e., Parent town hall forums, donuts with dads, muffins with moms, Watch Dog programs, etc.).
- Seek to listen to diverse perspectives of parents and families pertaining to the role they want the community to play in schools.
- Prioritize the relationship-building process to develop an understanding of the community's needs.
- Honor the ancestral knowledge and lived experiences of parents and families.
- Create committees that will allow parents, families, and community members to assist with oversight of school policies and practices.
- Advocate for community-based goals.[123]

---

[123] Ibid. p. 192.

A Vision for the Community

To hold us accountable for prioritizing family and community engagement, I encourage leaders to employ the V-Framework mentioned in Step 3. Remember, the V-Framework consists of three components: *Vision*, *Values*, and *Visible Evidence*. At a foundational level, every school should have a clear and concrete vision for family and community engagement. This vision should move beyond abstract ideas about family and community engagement to an actual plan for improving the school-community relationship. To begin the visioneering process that will ultimately lead to the creation of a plan, educators should ask the following questions:

- What should family and community engagement look like in our school or district?
- Which educators in our context will be necessary to the creation of a family and community engagement plan?
- What events or activities can we organize that are of interest and value to members of the community we serve?
- How can we ensure that we are employing a culturally responsive approach to family and community engagement?

Educators have to do more than talk about family and community engagement. We must use the highest level of intentionality to create a plan and map out the logistical steps necessary to effectively execute a family and community engagement plan. We must also organize a team of diverse individuals that includes school leaders, counselors, social workers, school psychologists, teachers, and others who have the best interest of the community in mind. As CREs, it is our responsibility to respond appropriately to the needs of our students, families, and community. Yet, this will never happen if we cannot envision the school playing a larger role in the overall health, wellness, and success of the communities we seek to serve.

Along with crafting a vision for enhancing the family, community, and school partnership, schools should identify values and key indicators that will serve as visible evidence for the prioritization of family and community engagement. These key indicators can help educators hold one another accountable. In addition, these key indicators can help schools approach family and community engagement in a more structured and strategic manner. According to Khalifa (2018), "School leaders must structure schools in ways that not only accommodate, but also incorporate and celebrate aspects of community."[124]

---

[124] Ibid. p. 40.

Evaluating Our Attempt to Prioritize the Community

We must ask ourselves a few questions about our attempts to build rapport with the community if we intend on prioritizing family and community engagement. Some questions include the following: How can we celebrate aspects of the community if we fail to see the inherent beauty within the community? How can we value the community if we view the community from a deficit perspective? How can we listen to members of the community if we have not invited them into the school, provided them with a seat at the table, and amplified their voices? What evidence do we have that would indicate that we have taken time to listen to the community? After we have answered a few self-reflective questions about our approach to prioritizing family and community engagement, we must commit to learning the community's story.

Learning the Community's Story

Educators must understand that every community has a story. Meaning there is a collective experience that members of a community share. For example, many communities of color continue to grapple with the aftermath of historical inequities such as redlining and other unfair housing practices. In an article titled "Redlining, Racism, and Food Access in US Urban Cores," Shaker et al. (2022)

highlighted how unfair housing practices of the 1930s have "caused persistent social, political, and economic problems for communities of color" (p.101).[125] According to Shaker et al., these policies, inspired by racist and xenophobic beliefs about communities of color, limited the community's access to quality foods which exacerbated food insecurity. Additionally, "redlining greatly constrained African Americans, other people of color, and immigrants from accessing capital and achieving social mobility gains."[126] Although redlining was officially prohibited in 1968, its legacy continues to impact communities of color.

Due to historical discrimination and other harmful practices perpetuated by systems targeting communities of color, it was only natural for these communities to develop a collective distrust for "systems." Consider the distrust for the criminal justice system that many communities of color share. This narrative has been created and sustained by the history of lynching, police brutality, sentencing disparities among racial groups for the same crimes, and many other apparent inconsistencies when it comes to the application of equity, equality, and justice. Many individuals within communities of color do not trust the housing system, the criminal justice system, the political system, or

---

[125] Shaker, Y., Grineski, S.E., Collins, T.W., & Flores, A. B. (2022). Redlining, racism and food access in US urban cores. *Agriculture and Human Values, 40*, 101–112. https://doi.org/10.1007/s10460-022-10340-3
[126] Ibid.

the educational system, just to name a few. Yet, educators sometimes expect communities of color to forget their historical experiences, let their "guard down," and commit to partnering with the educational system. This logic is flawed because many individuals within communities of color have also experienced injustices and marginalization in the context of schools.

When I was a special education teacher, I had a parent who refused to come into the school building to conduct an IEP meeting. She preferred phone conferences for every meeting, which was not a problem for me. Nevertheless, after years of working with this parent and developing a positive rapport with her son, I asked her why she refused to come to the school for an IEP meeting. I was genuinely curious because she was the only parent that I had never met face to face. She explained, "When I attended school as a student, I was treated horribly." She said, "The teachers and principals were so nasty to me that I vowed to never enter a school again." For this parent, school was a place that inflicted trauma upon her.

We must understand that stories like the parent who experienced trauma in school are not uncommon in communities of color. These historical narratives shared by members of a community can influence the community's willingness to interact with and embrace systems. Yes, the educational system is included in this notion. While it is certainly possible for systems to change over time, we must understand that memory is difficult to delete from the brain's software. Therefore, educators must seek to understand how collective experiences and shared narratives circulating within the community impact the school-community relationship.

Last year, I was engaging a principal in the Southeast region of Virginia in an executive coaching conversation about community engagement. This leader shared the following sentiment with me. She stated, "The other day, I received a phone call from a concerned parent who is considering enrolling her child in my school. The mother expressed that before she enrolled her child, she desired to meet with me because she had some questions about how parents are treated by staff in my building." The principal felt blindsided by the parent's remarks. Nevertheless, the principal proceeded to explain that the parent told her she read a post on a social media group page that mentioned the unfair treatment of parents at the school from five years ago. Since this principal was only in her second year as the leader of this school, she was upset that she inherited a narrative that she did not create or contribute to. With a grin and a reassuring tone, I said, "Welcome to school leadership in the age of social media."

Responding to the Community's Story

This account simply represents a microcosm of a much larger situation. Every leader in today's schools, and every educator for that matter, has inherited a narrative about the educational system that they may not have created. Regardless of this fact, educators have a responsibility to help change the narrative for many communities. This is exactly why educators must create opportunities for parents, families, and other members of the community to share their stories. It is imperative for leaders and educators to proactively help create new narratives within the community. However, these narratives cannot be shallow political statements. The principal should not simply seek to enter the community of marginalized families to pose for a quick photo op. Listening to the community's story in an attempt to prioritize family and community engagement must come from the heart.

This is why it is crucial for educators to do the inner work of fostering multicultural consciousness. By developing an awareness of self, knowledge of difference, and interpersonal disposition toward diversity, educators will be able to approach communities with empathy and compassion. Remember, attitudes and beliefs, whether implicit or realized, will always be made visible through one's actions. For this reason, it is essential for educators to see communities as assets to schools and schools as assets to communities.

School as a Community Asset

Listening to community perspectives is not only one of the best ways to gain an understanding of the community to dispel deficit thoughts and myths about the community, but it is also one of the best ways to identify opportunities for the school to serve as an asset to the community. Imagine a new paradigm for family and community engagement that centers the school as a unifying and empowering institution that maximizes the potential of individuals in and outside of the school walls. Imagine a place committed to helping families as much as it claims to be committed to helping children. Imagine a place strategically designed to collaborate with and support the community. While this may initially seem like a farfetched vision for a school, one principal has already prioritized family and community engagement to this level.

Principal Akbar Cook

Akbar Cook is a high school principal in Newark, New Jersey.[127] He has been featured on the Ellen

---

[127] Chakrabarti, M. (April 23, 2019). *High school principal brings free laundromat – And bullying relief – To students.* WBUR 2023. https://www.wbur.org/onpoint/2019/04/23/akbar-cook-new-jersey-principal-laundry-program

DeGeneres Show, and his school has been personally visited by Oprah Winfrey because of his innovative and community-centered approach. Principal Cook's school, West Side High School, is situated in a low-income community that is home to many diverse families. When he first arrived, he noticed that some of the violence from the community was negatively impacting students in his school. In an attempt to reduce the violence in his community, which he stated was mostly occurring between 6:00 PM and 11:00 PM, he created an after-school program called "Lights On."[128] The Lights On program allowed students to be cared for at the school site during those peak hours. Principal Cook opened the doors of the school and allowed the school to become an asset to the community. He has stated that his program has helped to reduce crime in his school and community.

Since West Side High School is situated in a food desert (an urban area that lacks access to affordable or good-quality fresh foods), Principal Cook provides students with fresh produce every Friday.[129] When the Covid-19 pandemic exacerbated food insecurity in his community, he was determined to teach his students about the field of agriculture. Currently, he is working to install greenhouses

---

[128] The Ellen Show. (2019). *Ellen meets extraordinary New Jersey principal Akbar Cook*. YouTube. https://youtu.be/O1P6oZjfR54
[129] Pix11 News. (2022). *Principal akbar's winning strategy in Newark*. YouTube. https://youtu.be/16_XT3ySOpE

on the campus of the high school so young people can learn how to grow their own food. He told a reporter that he is determined to help his community understand the principle of "how to fish instead of giving them fish."[130]

Not only did Principal Cook work out the logistics to extend the school hours and provide students with access to food, but he also acquired funding to install a "Laundry Room" on campus.[131] His laundry room contains several commercial washing machines and dryers that students can use to clean their clothes. According to Principal Cook, many of his students were missing school because they were being harassed and bullied for coming to school wearing clothes that were not clean. This unfortunate situation created an environment where many students felt psychologically and emotionally unsafe. As a result, Principal Cook was motivated to install a laundry room where students could wash their clothes free of charge.

Principal Cook has modeled for us how CREs can respond appropriately to the needs of students and the community-at-large. He has proved that it is possible to reimagine school as a resource and an asset for the community. Now, schools across the nation have started installing laundry machines on campuses situated in low-

---

[130] Ibid.
[131] CBS Mornings. (2019). *New Jersey principal opens school laundry room for his "babies."* YouTube. https://youtu.be(/BlrhR6TZphA

income areas.[132] According to Slater-Tate (2016), "Research from the 2016-2017 school year shows that high-risk students attended school nearly two more days a month while participating in the laundry program" (p.1).[133] These programs are not only found in all 50 states in the US but also across the world in Saudi Arabia, Ireland, and South Africa. If educators can conceive a compelling vision based on responding to the needs of parents and families, we can accomplish great things for students. This is what can happen when schools listen to the needs of the community and prioritize family and community engagement.

---

[132] Slater-Tate, A. (Aug 1, 2016). *Schools find one simple answer to attendance problem: Washing machines.* Today. https://www.today.com/parents/schools-find-one-simple-answer-attendance-problem-washing-machines-t101318

[133] Ibid., p. 1.

Summary of Step 4: Prioritizing Family and Community Engagement

Throughout this book, I have argued for an understanding of the historical context that the current educational system is situated. I have also discussed the need to develop multicultural consciousness as a prerequisite for applying culturally responsive practices. In step four, I argued that CREs also prioritize family and community engagement. This must become a goal for every school because the school-community relationship is a key factor in closing achievement gaps and increasing the academic performance of diverse students. While the process of prioritizing family and community engagement must start with school leaders, it should not stop with them. Every educator within the school must also prioritize family and community engagement as a necessary step in becoming culturally responsive.

I believe it is impossible to become a CRE while neglecting families and communities. Families and communities possess a wealth of knowledge and cultural insight that can help educators meet the unique needs of diverse students. Additionally, an effective family/community-school partnership can help debunk stereotypes and misinformed assumptions that serve as instructional barriers to academic excellence for many culturally diverse students. Without an attempt to gain accurate knowledge about the community's collective story, efforts to integrate students' culture into the curriculum will be inaccurate at best and biased at worst. CREs are educators who see the community as an asset to the school and the school as an asset to the community. For this reason, the goal of each school must be to become a culturally responsive learning institution. In support of culturally responsive schools, Brown (2007) argued that schools, as a whole, must "become culturally competent educational systems" (p. 61).[134]

Extension Questions for Leaders to Consider:

1. In what ways can your school become an asset for the community?
2. Do you have a vision and a concrete plan for improving family and community engagement in your school?
3. What will you do to amplify the voices of parents, families, and members of the community in which you serve?
4. Have you identified at least 3 core events/activities that your school can host to meet the needs of parents and families?

---

[134] Brown, M. R. (2007). Educating all students: Creating culturally responsive teachers, classrooms, and schools. *Intervention in School & Clinic, 43*(1). https://doi.org/10.1177/10534512070430010801

Extension Questions for Teachers to Consider:

5. Do parents believe teachers in your school value culturally and linguistically diverse students?
6. Do parents feel that teachers only call home to report behavioral issues?
7. How have educators communicated with parents to let them know that their input is valued? (i.e., emails, phone calls, Remind, YouTube Videos, surveys, interviews, etc.)

Step 5: Advocate for Culturally Responsive Schools

Step 5 - Advocate for Culturally Responsive Schools

*"Not everything that is faced can be changed;
but nothing can be changed until it is faced."*
- James Baldwin

"Schools (not children) must change."
- Jeffrey M. R. Duncan-Andrade

Essential Question: How can I help my school become a culturally responsive institution?

Culturally Responsive Advocacy

     The reality is no one will know what CREs stand for or oppose until CREs use their voices to express themselves. In this step, I argue that CREs must speak up and advocate for culturally responsive schooling. In a recent study, Warren-Grice (2017) utilized a qualitative methodology to capture the experiences and reflections of five Black educators who advocated for culturally responsive approaches in predominantly White suburban high schools.[135] Warren-Grice noted that the participants in

---

[135] Warren-Grice, A. (2017). Advocacy for equity: Extending culturally relevant pedagogy in predominantly White suburban schools. *Teachers College Record, 119* (1), 1-26. https://eric.ed.gov/?id=EJ1144289

the study used two forms of advocacy to help students of color, namely "racial advocacy" and "academic advocacy."[136]

Racial Advocacy

According to Warren-Grice (2017), racial advocacy occurs when "educators navigate and negotiate the racial space to challenge cultural-deficit beliefs and traditional White middle-class ideologies that inform teaching practices and policies."[137] While working with faculty and staff, the advocates engaged in racial advocacy in four ways:

1. They served as mediators to ensure that the school was treating students of color equitably.
2. They negotiated for increasing the number of Black students in Advanced Placement (AP) courses.
3. They led cultural workshops for faculty and staff to increase cultural competency in the school.
4. They "challenged staff members to make the curriculum more inclusive, with literature from diverse authors."[138]

In addition to supporting faculty and staff, the participants provided direct support to students. Warren-

---

[136] Ibid., p.1.
[137] Ibid., p.12.
[138] Ibid., p.14.

Grice (2017) explained, "These educators also sought to affirm students' identity and culture both individually and culturally."[139] They created afterschool programs that provided space for young people to discuss the beauty and brilliance of their cultural heritage. They also validated the unique racial experiences of students of color.[140] These educators created a safe space for culturally diverse students to be vulnerable about their lived experiences and personal struggles related to responding appropriately to racial microaggressions.

Academic Advocacy

In addition to supporting culturally diverse students' social and emotional needs, Warren-Grice explained that the participants engaged in academic advocacy to explicitly encourage students of color to reach their highest academic potential. They hosted individual and group mentoring and tutoring sessions. Moreover, they took students on "cultural field trips" and college visits. These educators were intentional about helping students embrace their racial and cultural identities while cultivating their academic skills. Students also had the option of attending "student life workshops," where they could learn how to write a resume, communicate effectively with

---

[139] Ibid., p.15.
[140] Ibid.

adults, prepare a four-year plan to attend college, navigate race-related conversations that may have come up at school or in the local or national news, and much more. In Warren-Grice's study, the educators intentionally elevated advocacy for culturally responsive approaches in their school context.

Why Were They Inspired to Become Advocates?

During interviews with the participants in the study, Warren-Grice learned that the educators felt it was their responsibility to engage in advocacy that included "protecting students of color on all fronts and from various forms of mistreatment, neglect, and macro and micro forms of racism in policies, curriculum, traditions, and teacher-student and student-student relations."[141] These educators also felt obligated to remove barriers that were blocking students of color from accessing AP courses. They were inspired to speak up because they believed advocating for culturally diverse students was their "responsibility and moral obligation."[142] Simply put, it was the right thing to do. Similar to the educators in Warren-Grice's study, every school needs culturally responsive advocates who work to address policies and practices that negatively impact culturally diverse students.

---

[141] Ibid., p.19.
[142] Ibid., p.18.

3 Areas Where Culturally Responsive Advocacy is Needed in Every School

Maybe you want to become a culturally responsive advocate, but you do not know where to start. In the next few pages, I will provide three areas where culturally responsive advocacy is needed in schools across the United States. In addition, I lay out a 7-point plan for culturally responsive advocacy that could serve as a template to help you get started in your local context.

#1 – Advocate for Equitable Discipline

Not only must CREs advocate for culturally responsive instruction, but they must also advocate for equitable discipline policies and practices. The reality is educators cannot effectively teach diverse students if they are constantly being removed from the instructional environment due to exclusionary discipline practices. As long as students of color continue to be excluded from the instructional setting due to inequitable disciplinary practices, achievement gaps will continue to widen. Unfortunately, racial disparities in school discipline have been a national concern for decades. It is well-known that students of color have been suspended more frequently and for longer durations than their White counterparts.

Flanery (2015) noted that Black students are three times more likely to be suspended and expelled than White students.[143] As reported by the Mid-Atlantic Equity Center (2016), almost 43,000 Black students were suspended from Virginia K-12 public schools in a single academic year.[144] Black students were only 24% of the student population in school districts across the state but comprised 51% of suspensions and 41% of expulsions (Mid-Atlantic Equity Center, 2016). These statistics have remained constant over the years. Despite the presence of racial disparities in school discipline across the U.S., there is no evidence that suggests African American students misbehave at a significantly higher rate when compared to other groups. If this is true, what is the cause of inequities in school discipline? The answer may be associated with implicit biases, stereotypical beliefs, and problematic perceptions of minoritized youth.[145] George (2015) stated:

> In the context of school discipline, race, and gender stereotypes particularly function to criminalize African American youth and to reinforce cultural beliefs about perceived inherent behavioral deficiencies and African

---

[143] Flannery, M. E. (2015). The school-to-prison pipeline: Time to shut it down. *NEA Today Magazine, 33*(1), 42–45. https://www.nea.org/advocating-for-change/new-from-nea/school-prison-pipeline-time-shut-it-down

[144] The Mid-Atlantic Equity Center. (2016). *Disproportionality in discipline of African American Males: Addressing critical equity issues.* https://maec.org/wp-content/uploads/2016/04/Disproportionality-in-Discipline-AfAm-Males.pdf

[145] George, J. A. (2015). Stereotype and school pushout: Race, gender, and discipline disparities. *Arkansas Law Review (1968-Present), 68*(1), 101–129. https://law.uark.edu/alr/PDFs/68-1/alr-68-1-101-129George.pdf

American cultural norms in need of 'social correction.' (p.102)

This is why CREs must advocate for equitable disciplinary practices. School discipline practices contribute to the school-to-prison pipeline and sustain the academic achievement gaps that CREs are working to close.

#2 – Advocate for Equitable Inclusion in Gifted Education

In many cases, culturally diverse students are unable to advocate for themselves, especially those in elementary schools. For decades, African American, Hispanic American, and other minoritized elementary students have been underrepresented in gifted and talented education programs.[146] This underrepresentation is not due to a lack of brilliance. No racial or cultural group has a monopoly on genius, and neither is any racial or cultural group inherently inferior. Yet, "several cultural matters that can hinder teachers' judgments and decisions in recruiting and retaining students of color in gifted programs" has been cited as the cause for this

---

[146] Speirs Neumeister, K.L., Adams, C., Pierce, R.L., Cassady, J.C., & Dixon, F.A. (2007). Fourth-grade teachers' perceptions of giftedness: Implications for identifying and serving diverse gifted students. *Journal for the Education of the Gifted, 30*(4), 479-499. https://files.eric.ed.gov/fulltext/EJ769920.pdf

discrepancy.[147] Milner and Ford (2017) alluded to the fact that African American and Hispanic American students tend to be underrepresented in gifted programs by 50% each (p.166). This exclusion from gifted programs should sound the alarm for advocates of culturally responsive education. Milner and Ford (2017) stated, "Teachers can be the voice that will not go away; they can insist that these students be better represented in such programs" (p.166). Therefore, CREs must advocate for the inclusion of culturally diverse youth in gifted programs as well as in rigorous courses in secondary schools.

According to The Education Trust (2020), Black and Latino students are unequally represented in advanced coursework.[148] Black students make up 15% of eighth graders, but only 10% of the students enrolled in Algebra 1 (a more advanced math class for middle school students). The same issue is impacting Latino students. Latino students comprise 25% of eighth graders but only 18% of those in advanced middle school math classes. This pattern of exclusion is also visible in the high school context. Black, Latino, and low-income students are

---

[147] Milner, H. R., & Ford, D. Y. (2007). Cultural considerations in the underrepresentation of culturally diverse elementary students in gifted education. *Roeper Review, 29*(3), 166-173.
https://doi.org/10.1080/02783190709554405
[148] The Education Trust. (2020, January 9). *Black and Latino students shut out of advanced coursework opportunities.*
https://edtrust.org/press-release/black-and-latino-students-shut-out-of-advanced-coursework-opportunities/

underrepresented in Advanced Placement (AP) courses.[149] According to Masters (2021), low-income students of all races and ethnicities are "four times less likely to take AP classes as their peers."[150] Therefore, CREs must speak up for the inherent brilliance of culturally diverse and minoritized youth because these students can certainly be successful in advanced courses when given the opportunity.

#3 – Advocate for Culturally Responsive Approaches in Special Education

While African American, Hispanic, and other minoritized students are underrepresented in gifted education and advanced coursework, they are often overrepresented in special education. According to Tefera and Fischman (2020), "Racial disproportionality in special education is an ongoing injustice in schools in the United States" (p. 434).[151] Interestingly, disproportionality is not found across all special education disability categories. It is predominantly found in categories that rely heavily on

---

[149] Ibid.
[150] Masters, K. (2021, April 28). *Black and low-income students are underrepresented in Virginia AP classes, report finds.* Virginia Mercury. https://www.virginiamercury.com/2021/04/28/black-and-low-income-students-are-underrepresented-in-virginia-ap-classes-report-finds/
[151] Tefera, A. A., & Fischman, G. E. (2020). How and why context matters in the study of racial disproportionality in special education: Toward a critical disability education policy approach. *Equity & Excellence in Education, 53*(4), 434–449. https://doi.org/10.1080/10665684.2020.1791284

teachers' observations and input. According to O'Connor and Fernandez (2006), "disproportionality plagues judgmental but not nonjudgmental categories of special education" (p. 6).[152] Judgmental categories refer to categories where educator discretion plays a major role in whether a student is found eligible for special education services. Nonjudgmental categories often require the attention and confirmation of medical professionals.

Judgmental categories include emotional disability, specific learning disability, and intellectual disability, whereas nonjudgmental categories include orthopedic impairments, visual impairments, deaf, blind, or other pronounced cognitive and psychological statuses. The U.S. Department of Education (2015) reported that nationally, Black students were more than twice as likely to be found eligible for special education services related to emotional disabilities and intellectual disabilities when compared to all other students.[153] Similarly, Native American students were twice as likely to be found eligible for having a specific learning disability. Data indicates that disproportionality thrives in subjective categories as opposed to objective categories. In other words, educators'

---

[152] O'Connor, C., & Fernandez, S. D. (2006), Race, class, disproportionality: Reevaluating the relationships between poverty and special education. *Educational Researcher, 35(*6), 6-11. https://doi.org/10.3102/0013189X035006006

[153] U.S. Department of Education (2015). 37th annual report to Congress on the implementation of the Individuals with Disabilities Education Act, 2015. Alexandria, VA: U.S. Department of Education.

discretion, attitudes, and beliefs could be contributing to the overrepresentation of minoritized students in special education. This is yet another reason for CREs to become advocates of culturally responsive schools in their local contexts. For those looking for a starting point for culturally responsive advocacy, I submit the following 7-point plan that can serve as a guide to help educators spark an introductory conversation. Here are 7 things CREs should advocate for within the context of schools.

7-Point Plan for Culturally Responsive Advocates

1. An asset-based understanding of students' cultures as opposed to deficit-based ideologies.
2. A student-centered approach to teaching and learning that centers students' culture, interests, and lived experiences.
3. Access to instructional resources and teaching materials that expose all students to multicultural contributions across the curriculum.
4. A concrete professional development plan that goes beyond "quick fixes." Educators need sustained training and coaching that will facilitate the development of appropriate attitudes, beliefs, and dispositions about culturally diverse students.
5. School as a space where students' cultures are sustained, caring relationships are nurtured, and high expectations are promoted for all learners.

6. A concrete family and community engagement plan containing goals for improving the relationship between the school and community.
7. A Culturally Responsive Committee (CRC) comprised of educators committed to the work of collaborating, learning, and growing in a genuine attempt to become CREs.

Culturally Responsive Schools and Advocacy

I believe advocacy must play a central role in the development of culturally responsive schools. In fact, I do not believe schools will become culturally responsive without advocates who are unapologetic about prioritizing the needs of culturally diverse learners. Educators who use their voices to speak up for culturally diverse youth and other marginalized students are essential to the work of educational equity. Therefore, the fifth and final step of becoming CREs is to advocate for culturally responsive schools. Students whose voices have historically been silenced need CREs to speak up on their behalf.

Summary of Step 5: Advocate for Culturally Responsive Schools

While it should be a personal goal for educators to become culturally responsive, collectively, we must also seek to create and multiply culturally responsive schools. This is the only way to provide a quality education for each child. As noted by Irvine and Armento (2001), "The school failure of culturally diverse students, particularly African American, Hispanic, and Native American students, is well documented" (p. 3). While this has been a common theme for most educational institutions of the past, it does not have to be a common theme for the future. We can change schools if we use our voices. We can improve outcomes for each student and close achievement gaps if we are willing to advocate for educational equity. It starts with us. Each educator across the United States must commit to becoming CREs who advocate for culturally responsive schools.

As mentioned in this step, culturally responsive advocates are needed to address discipline inequities facing diverse youth. Secondly, culturally responsive advocates are needed to call out and bring attention to the exclusion of diverse students in gifted programs and advanced courses. Thirdly, culturally responsive advocates are needed to address disproportionality in special education placement. For too many diverse students, special education becomes nothing more than a temporary holding cell that contributes to the school-to-prison pipeline. The issues hindering the academic success of students of color will only be disrupted by advocates of culturally responsive approaches to education.

Extension Questions for Educators to Consider:

1. What does Culturally Responsive Advocacy mean to you?
2. How might culturally responsive advocates be able to help improve student achievement?
3. On a scale from 1 (We have no issues) to 10 (We have major issues), how would you describe the need for culturally responsive advocates to speak up about inequities in discipline within your local context?
4. On a scale from 1 (We have no issues) to 10 (We have major issues), how would you describe the need for culturally responsive advocates to speak up about equitable inclusion in gifted programs and advanced coursework within your local context?
5. On a scale from 1 (We have no issues) to 10 (We have major issues), how would you describe the need for culturally responsive advocates to speak up about the overrepresentation of minoritized

students in special education within your local context?

6. Of the items listed in the "7-Point Plan for Culturally Responsive Advocates," which one stands out to you the most?
7. What will you do within your local context to advocate for culturally responsive schools and disrupt inequities facing diverse youth?

Section 3: Confidence and Culturally Responsive Self-Efficacy

Essential Question: Why is it imperative for educators to develop confidence and self-efficacy for teaching diverse students?

    One thing that I have learned from coaching and supporting educators in predominantly African American Title 1 schools is the fact that confidence is the "secret sauce." The problem is not all educators of culturally diverse students possess the confidence to reach these students. When I was a Title 1 Instructional Coach, a White female teacher entered my office, sat down with a dejected facial expression, and said, "Mr. Taylor, I need some help. I can't teach these children because I'm White." She was not the first White female teacher who felt comfortable and vulnerable enough with me to express this sentiment. From an instructional coach's perspective, I always explained that race does not dictate educator effectiveness.

    Children do not care about the color of their teacher's skin. The only thing students really want to know is, "Do you care about me, and can you help me succeed?" In other words, do you have the right pedagogical posture and instructional skillset to help students achieve their potential? For students, race is a non-factor. It does not matter what an educator looks like as long as they are competent, capable, and confident in their ability to inspire students to achieve at a high level. This is why helping educators develop confidence and improve their self-efficacy in regard to educating students of color is an educational imperative.

The impact of educator confidence on student outcomes has also been validated in educational research literature. According to Donohoo et al. (2018), "When the members of a team of educators are confident, they have the ability to make a difference in a school; it can have a significant impact on school culture and achievement" (p. 1).[154] Similar to how yeast causes bread to rise, confidence is the ingredient that causes educators to elevate their willingness to employ culturally responsive practices. Without confidence, educators will never develop the efficacy required to effectively execute tasks associated with culturally responsive approaches. If we fail to increase educator confidence and self-efficacy, culturally responsive practices will never be employed, and this amazing

---

[154] Donohoo, J., Hattie, J., & Eells, R. (2018, March 1). *The power of collective efficacy*. ASCD. https://www.ascd.org/el/articles/the-power-of-collective-efficacy

student-centered approach to increasing academic achievement for diverse learners will be reduced to a popularized educational buzzword. We cannot allow this to happen. Therefore, in this final section, I highlight the role confidence and self-efficacy play in becoming CREs.

Self-Efficacy and Teacher Efficacy

In 1977, Albert Bandura introduced a theoretical basis for the role attitudes and beliefs have on actions; this construct became known as self-efficacy.[155] According to Bandura, self-efficacy is defined as "beliefs in one's capabilities to organize and execute the courses of action required to produce given attainments" (p. 3). When this construct is applied to teaching, it is called teacher efficacy (Berman et al., 1977).[156] According to Berman et al. (1977), teacher efficacy is defined as "the extent to which the teacher believes he or she has the capacity to affect student performance" (p. 137). Research has shown that teachers' self-efficacy beliefs impact not only their ability to fulfill tasks associated with teaching (i.e., planning, organizing, and delivering instruction) but also their ability to meet the needs of their students. As educational

---

[155] Bandura, A. (1977). Self-efficacy: Toward a unifying theory of behavioral change. *Psychological Review, 84*(2), 191-215. https://psycnet.apa.org/doi/10.1037/0033-295X.84.2.191

[156] Berman, P., McLaughlin, M., Bass, G., Pauly, E., & Zellman, G. (1977). *Federal programs supporting educational change: Vol. VII. Factors affecting implementation and continuation* (Rep. No. R-1589/7-HEW). Rand. (ERIC Document Reproduction Service No. 140 432).

researchers became increasingly concerned with meeting the needs of culturally diverse students, the concept of self-efficacy and teacher efficacy would eventually be applied to meeting the needs of culturally diverse students. This led to the development of culturally responsive teaching self-efficacy (CRTSE) by Dr. Kamau Oginga Siwatu.

Culturally Responsive Teaching Self-Efficacy

Siwatu (2011) argued that individuals responsible for preparing educators must "nurture prospective teachers' culturally responsive teaching self-efficacy beliefs (CRTSE)" (p. 360).[157] According to Siwatu, CRTSE is defined as "an individual's belief in his or her capabilities to execute the practices associated with culturally responsive teaching" (p. 360). In other words, Siwatu believed that educators seeking to meet the needs of diverse learners must possess confidence in their ability to meet the needs of diverse learners. CRTSE is necessary for teachers in the general education setting as well as for teachers in the special education setting.

---

[157] Siwatu, K. O. (2011). Preservice teachers' culturally responsive teaching self-efficacy-forming experiences: A mixed-methods study. *The Journal of Educational Research, 104*(5), 360-369. https://doi.org/10.1080/00220671.2010.487081

CRTSE in Special Education

Chu (2011) examined the efficacy of in-service teachers of culturally diverse students with disabilities. She found that teachers who "rated high in both personal teaching efficacy and outcome efficacy were most likely to consider the general classrooms appropriate for a student with mild learning and/or behavior problems" (p. 7).[158] According to Chu, a strong relationship exists between teachers with higher efficacy and their ability to meet the needs of culturally diverse students with disabilities. In conclusion to her research study, Chu suggested that increasing teachers' CRTSE may help to reduce the overrepresentation of students of color in special education. In addition to the benefits noted by Chu (2011), Siwatu et al. (2011) explained, "There is mounting evidence that teacher self-efficacy beliefs are related to positive student and teacher outcomes" (p. 218). Therefore, educators committed to increasing their CRTSE beliefs will be in the best position to meet the needs of culturally diverse learners. This should be the goal for every educator.

---

[158] Chu, S. Y. (2011). Teacher perceptions of their efficacy for special education referral of students from culturally and linguistically diverse backgrounds. *Education, 132*(1), 3-14. https://doi.org/10.1177%2F0741932513520511

How Do We Increase Educator Efficacy?

My experiences as a special education teacher, Title 1 Instructional Coach, educational consultant, and researcher have made me a firm believer in dynamic professional learning opportunities. I honestly do not know any other way to increase educator confidence and efficacy outside of a sustained and job-embedded approach to adult learning. This is why I advocate for strategic and sequential professional development plans that are explicitly designed to increase educator self-efficacy. Educators must be guided by a 10-month professional development plan that includes access to reading materials, workshops, keynotes, job-embedded instructional coaching, podcasts, and other resources sequentially packaged as a roadmap to guide their journey to becoming CREs. This 10-month plan should function as a curricular framework and pacing guide for educators. Here is an example template of how a 10-month professional development plan might look:

Example Template - 10 Month PD Plan

Month	PD Objectives
August, September, and October	**Step 1 - Develop Historical Awareness** **Step 2 - Foster Multicultural Consciousness** As educators prepare for the new school year, they must be reminded of the following: 1) their PURPOSE and "WHY" as educators, 2) the vision, values, goals, and strategies for the school year, 3) the need to prioritize relationships with students, 4) the need to develop a structured learning environment, and 5) the rationale for culturally responsive practices.
November, December, January, February, and March	**Step 3 - Apply Culturally Responsive Approaches** **Step 4 - Prioritize Family and Community Engagement** After the initial wave of clarity and support is provided, reinforcement should be given via job-embedded coaching, PLCs, and other staff meetings. Educational leaders, academic coaches, specialists, consultants, and other support staff are vital during this time. Observations and coaching cycles should be used to ensure educators feel equipped to employ culturally responsive approaches to successfully meet the needs of culturally diverse learners.
April and May	**Step 5 - Advocate for Culturally Responsive Schools** Although testing will likely dominate as the topic of discussion during the last months of the school year, educators must be willing to use this time to reflect on their personal growth as CREs. Additionally, educators must reflect on the specific supports that were implemented to close achievement gaps. Honest, data-driven, and reflective conversations are mandatory at this time.

Purpose Pushers LLC 2023 | www.purposepushers.com | Dr. Jahkari Taylor

While some educators will "leap for joy" at the prospect of attending professional development designed to build their confidence and efficacy to effectively teach culturally diverse learners, many will choose to avoid these opportunities because they believe professional development focused on becoming CREs is unnecessary. I have heard countless educators say, "I don't need that stuff because it doesn't apply to me," "I know how to teach all children," "I'm not a new teacher," and "I've been doing this for a long time." Unfortunately, many educators are correct when they say they have been "doing this for a long time." This is precisely why the academic achievement gap between African American students and their White counterparts has been an issue on almost every measure of achievement in public education for nearly half a century (Williams, 2011).[159] At some point, educators must change their approaches to educating culturally diverse students. Every educator must commit to becoming CREs.

---

[159] Williams, A. (2011). A call for change: Narrowing the achievement gap between white and minority students. *The Clearing House, 84*(2), 65-71. https://doi.org/10.1080/00098655.2010.511308

Conclusion - Committing to the Process of Becoming Culturally Responsive Educators

Culturally responsive approaches have emerged in educational research as a valuable approach to increasing students' academic performance while enhancing their social-emotional skills. It generally focuses on centering students' culture in the academic space. Research shows that educators who utilize students' culture as an instructional tool can facilitate learning and successfully increase the academic achievement of culturally diverse students.[160] Researchers have also associated culturally responsive approaches with students experiencing increased friendship formation, prosocial interactions, acceptance of differences between peers, and support for others' learning (Abacioglu, 2020; Aronson & Laughter, 2016).[161] According to Abacioglu et al. (2020), culturally

---

[160] Gay, G. (2018). *Culturally responsive teaching*. Teachers College Press.
[161] Abacioglu, C. S., Volman, M., & Fischer, A. H. (2020). Teachers' multicultural attitudes and perspective-taking abilities as factors in culturally responsive teaching. *British Journal of Educational Psychology, 90*, 736-752. https://doi.org/10.1111/bjep.12328
Aronson, B., & Laughter, J. (2016). The theory and practice of culturally relevant education: A synthesis of research across content areas. *Review of Educational Research, 86*(1), 163-206. https://doi.org/10.3102%2F0034654315582066

responsive approaches have been "found to be related to positive student outcomes, such as increased student engagement, better achievement, and more positive peer relationships" (p. 737).

Additionally, Aronson and Laughter (2016) noted that culturally responsive approaches are associated with positive outcomes for students from many diverse cultural backgrounds (African Americans, Latinos, Mexicans, Puerto Ricans, Asians, Iraqis, other English language learners, and indigenous populations). Therefore, this approach is not just beneficial for one particular group of students. It is helpful for every student.

Transforming Lives Through Education

Howard (2020) argued that educators must "desire to empower students, and they must see themselves as transformative agents in that process" (p. 72.)[162] I believe CREs will be in the best position to adopt this mindset and accept the role as transformative agents of change for diverse learners across the United States. This is why I have argued that becoming CREs is necessary for each educator. Whether you are a principal, assistant principal, dean, teacher, counselor, coach, specialist, nurse, paraeducator, or other support staff within the school, the

---

[162] Howard, T. (2020). *Why race and culture matter in schools: Closing the achievement gap in America's classrooms.* Teachers College Press.

work of transforming lives in communities across our nation starts with you. Therefore, it is the responsibility of educators to commit themselves to the process of becoming CREs.

Students Deserve a Collective Commitment from Educators

While it is the responsibility of each educator to commit to becoming culturally responsive, the reality is students need educators to embrace a collective commitment to this work. It is not sufficient for students to have access to one or a few CREs in their school. They deserve access to CREs throughout the entirety of their public school experience. This will require a collective commitment from every educator.

John Hattie's (2016) work on *Visible Learning* has proved that collective teacher efficacy has a more powerful effect on student outcomes than any other factor.[163] In other words, even if a student's parents are not involved in their education, parental disengagement will not be more predictive of student outcomes than the educators tasked with teaching the student. For a reference to John Hattie's (2016) work, access the "Power of Collective Efficacy-Table" by utilizing the QR code in the back of this book.

---

[163] Hattie, J. (2016, July). *Mindframes and maximizers*. 3rd Annual Visible Learning Conference held in Washington, DC.

According to Donohoo et al. (2018), educators matter the most when predicting student achievement. Factors such as the student's socioeconomic status, home environment, motivation, ability to concentrate, and willingness to complete homework are not as powerful of a factor as the educators the student has access to.[164] Educators are literally difference makers for students. Therefore, it is imperative that each educator believes in their ability to make a difference in the lives of culturally diverse young people.

When every educator commits to the process of becoming CREs, we will see academic achievement increase for each student in public schools across our nation. I personally believe CREs will provide students with the best opportunities to reveal their brilliance to the world. This is because CREs lead with empathy and compassion while holding firm to high academic and behavioral expectations. They have a genuine and authentic love for humanity. They do not view diverse students' cultures from a deficit lens. In fact, they see students' cultures as an instructional tool and an asset to the learning community. In addition, CREs prioritize relationships with students to ensure that each child feels a strong sense of belonging in school. They seek to diversify their knowledge base to

---

[164] Donohoo, J., Hattie, J., & Eells, R. (2018, March 1). *The power of collective efficacy.* https://www.ascd.org/el/articles/the-power-of-collective-efficacy

increase their cultural competence, and they believe in the inherent brilliance of culturally diverse youth. Most importantly, they commit to the five necessary action steps outlined in this book.

Commitment to the Five Necessary Action Steps

Commitment #1: Develop Historical Awareness

CREs are defined by their commitments. First and foremost, they understand that the current educational landscape has been shaped by the past. This is why they are committed to developing historical awareness. CREs know that a more comprehensive understanding of the sociopolitical and historical context that the educational system is situated in is required to teach in this new current context. Additionally, they seek to develop historical awareness because they do not want to reproduce the historical oppressions that have defined American schooling of the past.

Commitment #2: Foster Multicultural Consciousness

Secondly, CREs desire to foster multicultural consciousness (awareness of self, knowledge of difference, and interpersonal disposition toward diversity). These educators understand that it is possible for good people to have biased attitudes about cultural diversity. Therefore, they seek to reflect on and critically examine their own lived experiences. The goal of this reflective exploration is to mitigate the impact of implicit biases, acknowledge cultural differences, and develop an interpersonal disposition toward diversity.

Commitment #3: Apply Culturally Responsive Approaches

Thirdly, CREs seek to ensure that the language associated with becoming culturally responsive is not reduced to a popularized buzzword. They do this by actively applying culturally responsive approaches across the school context. They hold themselves accountable by 1) drafting a concrete vision for culturally responsive practices in their school, 2) identifying and adopting culturally responsive values to govern behavior, and 3) ensuring that visible evidence of culturally responsive practices is identifiable in the school. Additionally, CREs seek to ensure students are immersed in a culturally responsive atmosphere that offers access to culturally responsive instructional resources. They also utilize encouraging communication while delivering dynamic, student-centered instruction.

Commitment #4: Prioritize Family and Community Engagement

CREs commit to prioritizing family and community engagement. They have the desire and capacity to envision a successful partnership between the school and the community characterized by collaboration and teamwork. They do this by creating opportunities to learn the community's story with the goal of amplifying the community's voice. This is fueled by their perspective of the community as an asset to the school and the school as an asset to the community.

Commitment #5: Advocate for Culturally Responsive Schools

Lastly, CREs intentionally speak up for diverse students and other marginalized youth. They seek to do what is right for children, and they view educational advocacy as a moral responsibility. CREs are the educators who will analyze and disaggregate data to ensure culturally diverse students are receiving equitable opportunities to thrive in school. They will speak up if diverse students are excluded from gifted and talented programs and other rigorous academic opportunities. In addition, they will voice their concerns if they notice disproportionality in discipline and the overrepresentation of diverse students in special education. CREs cannot turn a blind eye to harmful educational policies, practices, and other inequities that hinder the achievement of culturally diverse students.

Meet the Author
Dr. Jahkari "JT" Taylor

The images above speak for themselves. The picture on the left depicts a ninth grader who had a cumulative grade point average of 0.75. He skipped school every other Friday and accumulated 14 unexcused absences because socializing and surviving were more of a priority than academic success. The picture on the right illustrates the impact of educators who refused to give up on the student on the left. This is why I am extremely passionate about helping educators become CREs. I have not only researched the benefits of becoming CREs from a theoretical standpoint, but I have also experienced it on a personal level as well. I went from failing in high school to earning my Ph.D. because of the unconditional love of my mother and the determination of a few CREs who believed in my inherent brilliance and untapped potential. These educators altered the trajectory of my life. For this reason, I am forever grateful, inspired, and determined to reproduce transformational results for diverse young people in schools across the world. #OnPurpose

My Biography

Dr. Jahkari "JT" Taylor is an award-winning educational leader, researcher, author, and national speaker. He has over 16 years of experience working in the K-12 public school system as a Special Education teacher, Title 1 Instructional Coach, and full-time Educational Consultant.

JT has presented at the national conferences of many professional organizations, including the Association for Supervision and Curriculum Development (ASCD), the National Council of Teachers of English (NCTE), the Association for Middle Level Education (AMLE), and Learning Forward. JT has been featured in a WHRO Pubic Media commercial titled "The Teaching Profession" and has presented at K-12 schools, colleges, and universities across the nation. He has won numerous awards throughout his career, including Iota Phi Lambda Emerald Educator, Teacher of the Year at Oscar F. Smith High School, Overall City-Wide Teacher of the Year for Chesapeake Public Schools, and 2019 ASCD Emerging Leader. In 2021, JT was selected as one of Inside Business' 'Top 40 Under 40' in the Hampton Roads region of Virginia for exemplifying success in business and commitment to community service.

    JT aims to develop educator confidence and competence through dynamic professional learning opportunities to help educators move toward educational equity. His research focus includes culturally responsive teaching, Title 1 school improvement, special education, and parent and family engagement.

    JT can be reached at purposepushers.com or on social media platforms @purposepushers.

Downloadable Images, Diagrams, and Frameworks

Visit the following link or utilize the QR Code below to access each of the images, diagrams, and frameworks from this book.

http://bit.ly/BecomingCREDownloads

Made in the USA
Columbia, SC
11 April 2024